FIFTY YEARS
of
NAVAL TUGS

Bill Hannan

£4.95

List of abbreviations:—

A/C	Aircraft
BBV	Balloon Barrage Vessel
BDO	Boom Defence Officer
BHP	Brake Horse Power
BPF	British Pacific Fleet
BRNO	British Resident Naval Officer
CD	Captain of Dockyard
CE in C	Civil Engineer in Chief
C in CBPF	Commander in Chief British Pacific Fleet
C in CEI	Commander in Chief East Indies
CP	Captain of Port
C & M	Care and Maintenance
DAS	Director of Armament Supply
DBD	Director Boom Defence
DNAW	Director Naval Air Warfare
D of S	Director of Stores
D of ST	Director of Sea Transport
D of V	Director of Victualling
FO	Flag Officer
HLD	Harbour Launch (Diesel)
FOIC	Flag Officer in charge
IHP	Indicated Horse Power
MOT	Ministry of Transport
MOWT	Ministry of War Transport
NASO	Naval Armament Stores Officer
NOIC	Naval Officer in charge
RNAD	Royal Naval Armament Depot
RNO	Resident Naval Officer
SASO	Superintendent Armament Stores Officer
SBNO	Senior British Naval Officer
SCE	Superintendent Civil Engineer
SNONI	Senior Naval Officer N. Ireland
SNSO	Superintendent Naval Stores Officer
SORF	Senior Officer Reserve Fleet
SVSO	Superintendent Victualling Stores Officer

AUTHOR'S NOTE

Unfortunately, this book cannot be offered as a totally complete and accurate list of naval support tugs to operate over the last fifty years. It is based mainly on old records kept by the Director of Marine Services (Navy)—to whom I am indebted for access to them. I am particularly indebted to Messrs Quayle and Carey on his staff for their help and forbearance.

These old records, apparently started in 1946, were not kept for the purpose I used them and are therefore not as complete or as accurate as could be desired for the production of this book. Added to this is some personal knowledge and a little help from my friends—even so there are shortcomings as can be expected in a book for which little resource material is available. For these I apologise in advance. However, it serves to show the number and types of tugs which exist, and which have existed, over the years plus some indication of where they served and what happened to them.

My thanks also to Messrs J J Colledge, M J Gaston, P Thomas, E W Shannon, R Dennison, F Melville, S Goodman, M Lennon and many others who by correspondence have helped fill "gaps" in the production of this book.

I trust you enjoy the end result.

W J Harman.

CRAFTHOLE
TORPOINT

THE ROYAL MARITIME AUXILIARY SERVICE

With the exception of HMS WAKEFUL, which is not operated wholly as a RN tug, and CLARE which is manned by the Royal Navy at Hong Kong, all tugs in our naval service today are manned by members of the Royal Maritime Auxiliary Service. This service is headed by the Director of Marine Services (Navy) at Bath but local administration and operation of vessels is controlled by Captains of Ports and Queen's Harbour Masters (CPs and QHMs). Prior to 1958 these officers were known as Captains of Dockyards and King's/Queen's Harbour Masters (CDs and K/QHMs).

Until 1959 the large fleet of civilian manned auxiliary vessels necessary to support the Royal Navy in all its activities was managed and operated by the various departments in dockyards and naval bases. This large variety of craft, some designed for seagoing, some for purely harbour work and many for both purposes, were known simply as "Yardcraft".

Captains of Dockyards and King's/Queen's Harbour Masters and their equivalents in smaller ports who were responsible for ships' movements, operated the majority of tugs. However, some tugs, employed mainly on sea going duties, were manned by the Royal Navy (on a reducing basis after World War II) and some by civilians on Royal Fleet Auxiliary conditions of service. A few of the smaller tugs were operated by the Navy's supply departments—mainly for towing lighters.

In 1959 in the interest of greater efficiency and economy it was decided that all Yardcraft should be brought under one authority and the Port Auxiliary Service (PAS) was formed.

On 1 October 1976 this amalgamation was carried a stage further by the addition of other vessels in government service including those civilian manned tugs under Royal Fleet Auxiliary conditions of service. The PAS then became the RMAS.

Thus, during their lives, tugs could have been manned by the Royal Navy, civilians under RFA conditions, Yardcraft personnel, the Port Auxiliary Service or the Royal Maritime Auxiliary Service. Some tugs during wartime were requisitioned with their crews and these are briefly mentioned.

RMAS vessels are easily distinguished today by their black hulls, with white line at main deck level, buff superstructure and buff funnels with black tops. Pennant numbers are painted in white on black hulls or in black on buff where appropriate. They wear the Blue Ensign defaced in the fly by a yellow anchor over two yellow wavy lines.

Officers of the RMAS are known as Marine Services Officers with ranks afloat as follows:—

MSO 1

MSO 2

MSO 3

MSO 4

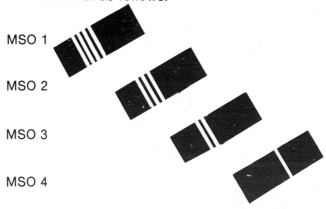

Engineer Officers are distinguishable by purple bands between their gold stripes.

Vessels may be commanded by any of the above ranks depending on the degree of responsibility needed.

Handling a wide variety of tugs develops skills not normally required by other ship Masters. As well as handling their own vessels (often in close proximity to others) Masters have to "double think" for the vessel they are towing and, with so much shiphandling experience, tend naturally to become good pilots.

Generally, the Masters of the larger tugs usually employed on ships' movements are qualified pilots for the ports in which they serve. They are distinguishable when qualified pilots by their cap badges. The normal RMAS officer's cap badge contains the RMAS flag surrounded by laurels and surmounted by a crown. In the pilot's badge the Blue Ensign is replaced by the flag of the Queen's Harbour Master which is a Union Jack with a white border (the Pilot Jack) containing in its centre a crown with the letters QHM beneath it.

Tug Design . . .

One important aspect of tug design worth mentioning is the fact that a tug must be able to turn easily whilst towing and this means, in the conventional tug, that the towing hook is

5

positioned at or near the natural pivoting point of the tug. As a result of this, a dangerous situation can arise during towing operations when the towing hawser is at right angles to the tug and for reasons not always under control of the Tug Master, the pull on the towing hawser increases and makes it impossible for the tug to manoeuvre. The tug is then pulled over on its side and is said to be 'Girded'. Tugs and crews have been lost under these circumstances and steps have been taken to reduce this inherent risk.

Early tugs' towing hooks were of simple design and from which tows could not be slipped. These were replaced by hooks from which a tow could be slipped—but this meant removing keep pins from the hooks while under strain—finally striking a part of the hook with a large hammer. This was extremely dangerous for the man carrying out the operation and in later tugs was replaced by power operated hooks remotely controlled.

The Clyde Towing Co introduced the Clyde Towing Arm which effectively placed the towing hook at the end of a rigid arm and these can best be seen in the photographs of Improved GIRL class tugs. Although the initial effect of the side pull on the girded tug would be to tilt her towards the tow, the consequent downswing of the towing arm would be checked by the pull of the towing hawser and tend to keep the tug upright.

In the more modern tugs improved steering with twin rudders, more powerful engines and quicker manoeuvring controllable pitch propellers have allowed the towing hooks to be positioned a little further aft. The problem of girding does not arise at all in the Tractor tugs where the propulsion units are forward in the tug with the towing hook right aft. If the tow overcomes these tugs they are merely towed by the stern in far less danger.

Bollard Pull is shown in the text (where known). This is measured by the tug towing against a spring balance secured ashore to a bollard using a towing hawser long enough to ensure that propeller wash does not reach the shore and effect results.

HM Tug Recovery (1953)

PILOT CLASS

Ship	Pennant Number	Completion Date	Builder
ALLIANCE	W77	1910	Chatham Dockyard
ATLAS	W41	1909	" "
PILOT	W03	1909	" "
ROVER (ROLLICKER) (RECOVERY)	W21	1909	" "

Length 153' 3" **Beam** 27' 5" **Draught** 14' **Displacement** 615 tons **Speed** 11 Knots **Engines** Steam reciprocating—coal fired (95 tons)—2 boilers. **IHP** 1400 **Propulsion** Twin screw—single rudder **Bollard Pull** Approx 14 tons **Range** 950 miles **Complement** 20.

HM Tug Alliance at Hong Kong (1939)

Notes

These vessels did quite a lot of sea towing and target towing although they were not fitted with towing winches. Rather narrow for their length, were slow to manoeuvre, but nevertheless were useful tugs.

For many years ATLAS and RECOVERY were easily recognised by the long spurs fitted to the top of their funnels to carry the aerials. The radio room was situated just aft of the funnel.

PILOT and ALLIANCE were fitted with upper bridges.

ALLIANCE was fitted with a 100 ton fresh water tank for issuing water to ships. Based Hong Kong manned by UK Yardcraft Officers and locally entered crew. Lost 19.12.41.

ATLAS was also fitted with the 100 ton fresh water tank. Based under CD Devonport after service in Hong Kong. 15.6.53 at Portsmouth for Coronation Review. 1958 Replaced by FAITHFUL. 21.5.58 sold to Lloyds, Albert Yard, Southampton.

PILOT, based at Portland. 23.3.60 sold to H G Pounds, Portsmouth. 27.3.60 arrived in New Waterway having been re-sold to Dutch shipbreakers.

ROVER became ROLLICKER and finally in 1934 RECOVERY. 15.6.53 at Portsmouth for Coronation Review. January 1958 sold for scrap to Haulbowline Industries Ltd, Passage West, Co Cork, Ireland.

TERRIER CLASS

Ship	Comp Date	Builder
TERRIER	1911	Alex Hall & Co Ltd, Aberdeen
TYKE	1913	Montrose SY

Length 75′ 6″ **Beam** 18′ 3″ **Draught** 9′ 6″ **GRT** 95 **Engines** Steam compound **IHP** 300 **Speed** 10 Knots **Propulsion** Single screw.

Notes
TERRIER—based Chatham as basin tug. 15.3.48 Sold to Messrs J P Knight.
TYKE—based Chatham as basin tug. July 1947 for disposal.

"R" CLASS

Ship	Pennant Number	Completion Date	Builder
RESOLVE	W85	1918	Ayrshire DY Co
RESPOND	W92	1918	" "
RETORT	W84	1918	Day, Summers & Co
ROLLICKER	W95	1918	Ferguson Bros
ROYSTERER	W91	1919	Thorneycroft

Length 186′ **Beam** 36′ 2″ **Draught** 17′ **Displacement** 1400 tons **Speed** 14 knots **Engines** Steam Reciprocating **Fuel** Coal capacity 270 tons—4 boilers—12 fires. Twin funnels **IHP** 2400 **Propulsion** Twin screws—single rudder **Bollard Pull** Approx 24 tons **Range** 2450 miles **Complement** 30.

Notes

RETORT and RESOLVE differed from the others of the class in having no forecastle. The fore deck was at main deck level. Excellent tugs both for harbour and sea work. Unfortunately they were not fitted with towing winches or even spring loaded towing hooks. The length and combination of a sea tow had therefore to be decided beforehand and could not afterwards be easily changed. The towing gear had to be long enough, heavy enough and with a deep enough catenary to absorb the effects of wave motion on the two vessels. In these tugs it usually consisted of wire from the towing hook to just clear of the stern then 100 fathoms of Manilla rope 21″ in circumference, then 100 fathoms or more of wire to the tow. These would be shackled together with heavy swivels between rope and wire to allow the rope to turn as it stretched. Needless to say that when such a tow came to an end and the gear had to be recovered it was a job for all hands—and the cook! 21″ Manilla rope when wet could be very stiff indeed needing several men to bend it around a winch drum. Even when harbour towing 20″ Manilla rope was used for towing ahead of large ships and again all hands were required to recover the tow.

Modern man-made fibre ropes and towing winches now make light and quick work of these once laborious tasks.

HM Tug Resolve (1924)

HM Tug Roysterer (towing HMS Eridge at Alexandria)

RESOLVE based Portsmouth Dockyard under CD. 22.9.50 sold to Messrs James Scott & Co Ltd.

RESPOND based Malta Dockyard under CD. 1943-46 transferred to Alexandria, 1956 sold at Malta & scrapped in Italy.

RETORT based Devonport Dockyard under CD until 1952 when she was given new boilers and transferred to Gibraltar. January 1958 replaced by CONFIDENT. 19.9.58 sold for £11,659-2-2.

ROLLICKER based Gibraltar under CD. Transferred to Nigerian Government but re-acquired by Admiralty in 1934. 3.6.52 sold at Gibraltar to British Iron & Steel Corporation (Salvage) Ltd for breaking up.

ROYSTERER based Malta Dockyard under CD. 1943-1946 transferred to Alexandria, 22.12.54 sold to Fratell Trafinetti. Genoa.

Livery for RESPOND and ROYSTERER based in the Mediterranean was red hull with white line at main deck level—white boats and superstructure. Buff funnels and masts. A further tug of this class ROLLCALL (W81) was built by Ferguson, sold on 16.8.22 and renamed ROMSEY.

SAINT CLASS

A class of 46 vessels built 1918/19 by various yards. Many of them were sold or transferred to the Canadian, New Zealand and Australian governments or the Spanish, Brazilian and Iraqi navies. Others were sold to commercial ports such as Shanghai, Sydney and Fremantle. Some of those sold were recalled for service in World War II.

The following were in naval service during the last 50 years:-

Ship	Pennant Number	Completion Date	Builder
SAINT ABBS	W02	1918	Ferguson Bros, Port Glasgow
SAINT ANNE	W36	1919	" "
SAINT ARVANS	WO5	1919	Day, Summers & Co Ltd. Southampton
SAINT AUBIN	W18	1918	Harland & Wolff, Govan
SAINT BLAZEY	W46	1919	Cran & Somerville
SAINT CLEARS	W06	1919	Livingstone & Cooper
SAINT CYRUS	W47	1919	Crichton & Co, Chester
SAINT DAY	W55	1918	Taikoo Dockyard Co, Hong Kong
SAINT DOGMAEL	W66	1918	" " "
SAINT DOMINIC		1919	Hong Kong & Whampoa Dockyard
SAINT ERTH		1919	Murdock & Murray
SAINT EWE		1919	" "
SAINT FAGAN	W74	1919	Lytham Shipbuilding Co
SAINT FERGUS (SAINT BONIFACE)	W04	1919	Fleming & Ferguson
SAINT GILES	W96	1919	Ferguson Bros, Port Glasgow
SAINT ISSEY	W25	1918	Napier & Miller, Glasgow
SAINT JAMES (SAINT BREOCK)	W56	1919	Hong Kong & Whampoa Dockyard
SAINT JUST	W90	1918	Napier & Miller, Glasgow

SAINT MABYN	W09	1919	Livingstone & Cooper
SAINT MARTIN	W27	1919	" "
SAINT MELLONS	W81	1918	Harland & Wolff, Govan
SAINT MINVER		1919	Day, Summers & Co, Southampton
SAINT MONANCE	W63	1919	Hong Kong & Whampoa Dockyard
SAINT OLAVES	W40	1919	Harland & Wolff, Govan
SAINT OMAR	W34	1919	Ferguson Bros, Port Glasgow
SAINT SAMPSON	W26	1919	Hong Kong & Whampoa Dockyard

Length 135' 6" **Beam** 29' **Draught** 14' 6" Max **Displacement** 860 tons **Speed** 12 knots **Engines** Steam reciprocating. Triple expansion **Fuel** Coal 240 tons **IHP** 1250 **Propulsion** Single Screw.

Notes

SAINT ABBS 1934 based Portsmouth. 1.6.40 lost by Bombing at Dunkirk.

SAINT ANNE 10.1922 sold to R MacGregor. Served with Royal Canadian Navy in World War II. 1943 renamed CASCAPEDIA.

SAINT ARVANS 25.8.23 sold to J H Clarke and renamed OCEAN EAGLE. 1941-44 served with Royal Canadian Navy.

SAINT AUBIN 12.4.24 sold to Shanghai Tug and Lighter Co. January 1940 recalled for naval service and served as a minesweeper on the China station until September 1941, then to Red Sea. 21.10.46 returned to owners, 1947 renamed TSZE HONG.

SAINT BLAZEY Dockyard tug at Bermuda. 12.7.46 sunk as a target off Bermuda.

SAINT CLEARS Based Sheerness Dockyard with Yardcraft crew. Served in evacuation of Dunkirk 1948 sold to Risdon Beasley.

SAINT CYRUS 1934 on Fleet Target Service with the Home Fleet. 22.1.41 lost, mined off the Humber.

SAINT DAY 1934 based Gibraltar. 1945-47 Fleet Tug, Malta. May 1947 paid off at Portsmouth—the last coalfired tug manned by the RN. 9.4.48 sold and renamed URSUS. 1962 renamed SAN CIRIACO.

HMS St Cyrus—note the side screens fitted when sailing from Devonport to Gibraltar.

SAINT DOGMAEL 1934 at Simonstown on Dockyard service. 1947 relieved by BRITON. October 1950 sold.

SAINT DOMINIC 12.11.19 sold at Hong Kong. 1939 recalled for war service. 8.12.41 lost in the China Sea, cause unknown.

SAINT ERTH September 1925 sold and renamed HEROS. 1940-46 served with the Royal Australian Navy.

SAINT EWE 11.10.26 sold to Iraq and renamed ALARM. 1939 hired by RN. 1942 renamed ALARM II. 1946 returned.

SAINT FAGAN 1934 on Fleet Target Service attached to HMS EXCELLENT, Portsmouth. 1.6.40 lost by bombing at Dunkirk.

SAINT FERGUS (later SAINT BONIFACE) 18.3.25 transferred to the New Zealand Government. 15.4.26 renamed TOIA. 1939-47 with R N Zealand Navy. 1955 sold.

SAINT GILES July 1922, sold and renamed KHALIFA. 1939-46 hired by Royal Australian Navy as SAINT GILES.

SAINT ISSEY 1934 on Fleet Target Service, Malta. 28.12.42 sunk by U617 off Benghazi.

SAINT JAMES (later SAINT BREOCK) Based China Station as dockyard tug. 14.2.42 lost, bombed by Japanese aircraft off Sumatra.

SAINT JUST 1934. On Fleet Target Service with Home Fleet. 1939 based Singapore. 14.2.42 sunk by Japanese aircraft in Durian Straits, Singapore.

HM Tug St Monace at Hong Kong (1939).

HM Tug St Breock

SAINT MABYN 1919 laid up 3.5.26 sold and renamed CAROLINE MOLLER. Recalled for war service. 7.10.42 lost, torpedoed by an E-boat in the North Sea.

SAINT MARTIN 1934 based Portsmouth on Fleet Target Service for HMS EXCELLENT. 21.5.46 paid off. November 1946 sold.

SAINT MELLONS Based Portsmouth Dockyard. July 1949 sold to H G Pounds and broken up at Portsmouth.

SAINT MINVER Laid up 23.4.25 sold to France as ABEILLE 22. 3.7.40 seized at Plymouth for war service. 1945 returned. 1951 scrapped.

SAINT MONANCE Based Hong Kong, manned by UK Yardcraft Officers and local crew. 28.12.45 at Alexandria. 15.7.46 paid off and destored. April 1948 sold.

SAINT OLAVES 22.6.22 sold. December 1939 recalled for war service. 21.9.42 lost, wrecked near Duncansby Head.

SAINT OMAR Based Gibraltar Dockyard. 6.11.47 sold at Gibraltar.

SAINT SAMPSON 8.6.22 sold. February 1940 hired by RN for war service. 7.3.42 foundered in Red Sea.

Other tugs of this class were:-

SAINT ARISTELL Built by Crabtree 1919. Sold to J Brown, Newcastle NSW.

SAINT ATHAN (W40) Built by Day, Summers 17.11.24. Sold to British Tanker Co.

SAINT BEES (W23) Built by Harland & Wolff 1922. Sold to Moller Towage Ltd. Renamed HENRY BURTON.

SAINT BOSWELLS (W51) Built by Cran & Somerville 1919. Mined 12.6.20 off Terschelling.

SAINT BOTOLPH (W34) Built by Livingstone & Cooper 1918. Sold to G Maclean 29.12.26. Renamed KUMAKI.

SAINT CATHERINE (W44) Built by Livingstone & Cooper 1919. Sold to A H Reid Vancouver. Renamed CANADIAN NATIONAL No 2.

SAINT CLEMENT Built by Ferguson 1919. 1921 Sold to Spain. Renamed CICLOPE.

SAINT COLUMB Built by Crichton 1918. 16.1.20 wrecked at Malta. Wreck sold to V Grech Ltd.

SAINT FAITH Built by Lytham SB 1919. Sold to Crichton Thompson 1921.

SAINT FINBARR (W22) Built by Fleming & Ferguson 1919. 1923 sold to Canadian Government. Renamed FRANKLIN.

SAINT FLORENCE Built by Crichton 1919. 14.11.24 sold to Canadian Pacific Railway. Renamed KYUQUOT.

SAINT GENNY (W04) Built by Crichton 1919. 12.1.30 foundered off Ushant whilst towing HMS SNAPDRAGON in company with SAINT CYRUS.

SAINT HELIERS (W08) Built by Ferguson 1919. 23.6.20 sold to Crichton Thompson.

SAINT HILARY Built by Lytham SB 1919. Sold to Waratah Tug & Salvage Co.

SAINT KEYNE Built by Murdoch & Murray 1919. 18.6.26 sold to Brazil. Renamed TIMES then ANNIBAL MENDOZA.

SAINT KITTS Built by Murdoch & Murray 1919. Sold to Adelaide SS Co. Renamed VCO.

SAINT MARY (SAINT CLAUDE) Built by Livingstone & Cooper 1919. Sold to J Fenwick, Sydney NSW. Renamed LINDFIELD.

SAINT OSYTH (SAINT ENODER) Built by Day, Summers 1919. 9.6.25 sold to Denmark. Renamed GARM.

SAINT TEATH Built by Walker 1919. 2.6.26 sold to Brazil. Renamed PARANA.

SAINT TUDY Built by Walker 1919. Sold to F P Barney, later renamed SAINT EILEEN.

Of the total of 64 tugs ordered the following 18 were cancelled:-
SAINT ALBERT, SAINT AUSTELL, SAINT BONIFACE, SAINT BREOCK, SAINT BRIDGET, SAINT BUDEAUX, SAINT CLAUDE, SAINT ENODER, SAINT ETIENNE, SAINT FINELLA, SAINT GERVAIS, SAINT GRACE, SAINT GREGORY, SAINT KEVERNE, SAINT OWEN, SAINT PHILIP, SAINT ROCHE, SAINT ROLLUX.

WEST CLASS

Ship	Comp Date	Builder
WEST ACRE	1919	Yarwood & Sons, Northwich
WEST BAY	1919	" "
WEST COCKER	1919	Philip & Son Ltd, Dartmouth
WEST CREEK	1918	Yarwood & Sons, Northwich
WEST DEAN	1919	Philip & Son Ltd, Dartmouth
WEST HYDE	1919	Crabtree

Length 89' **Beam** 21' **Draught** 10' 5" **GRT** 138 **Speed** 9 knots **Engines** Steam Recip **IHP** 450 **Propulsion** Single Screw **Complement** 3 Officers 6 ratings.

Notes

WEST ACRE—based Portsmouth with Naval Stores Department as C9 until 3.6.48 then to CD Portsmouth. 3.5.50 sold to Messrs E Handcock (1929) Ltd Cardiff. 1960 sold again and renamed LAVEROCK.

WEST BAY—based RNAD Priddys Hard, Portsmouth until 10.7.46 when she was put in C & M. 23.7.53 sold and renamed LARKSPUR.

WEST COCKER—based Chatham and Malta. 9.4.42 sunk by aircraft at Malta.

WEST CREEK—based Sheerness. 1949 sold and renamed MARGARET LAMEY.

WEST DEAN—based Upnor Chatham and Malta. 28.4.42 sunk by aircraft 28.4.42 at Malta.

WEST HYDE—based Chatham under CD. 23.8.47 for disposal, 1948 sold and renamed SEASIDER.

POULTRY CLASS

Ship	Comp Date	Builder
ANCONA	1919	H Scarr & Co, Hull
COCHIN	1919	Yarwood & Sons, Northwich
WYANDOTTE	1919	Rowledge, IW

Length 75' **Beam** 15' 8" **Draught** 7' 6" **GRT** 65 **Speed** 8.5 Knots **Engines** Steam Compound **IHP** 185 **Propulsion** Single Screw **Complement** 2 Officers 5 ratings.

Notes
ANCONA Based at Upnor, Chatham. 1946 sold.
COCHIN Based at Bull Point, Plymouth. 20.2.47 sold to Anglo Danubian Transport Co Ltd.
WYANDOTTE Based Chatham under CD until 1947 when transferred to CE in C as W74. 1948 sold to Messrs T Ward, Grays, Essex for breaking up.
Another tug of this class LEGHORN was based at Devonport but was not operational in the last 50 years.

BURN CLASS

Ship	Comp Date	Builder
BUCKIE BURN	1919	McGregor, Kirkintilloch
RATHVEN BURN	1920	" "

Length 72' **Beam** 17' 2" **Draught** 6' **GRT** 51 Knots **Engines** Steam Compound. Coal fired. **IHP** 200 **Propulsion** Single screw.

Notes
BUCKIE BURN The only Admiralty tug in Rosyth between 1935 and 1940. 14.9.58 sold to Messrs Brunton Ltd for scrap.
RATHVEN BURN Based Portsmouth. Basin tug. 3.6.52 sold to British Iron & Steel Corporation.

BRIGAND CLASS

Ship	Pennant Number	Completion Date	Builder
BANDIT (BRITON)	W69	1938	Fleming & Ferguson, Paisley
BRIGAND	W83	1937	" "
BUCCANEER	W49	1937	" "
FREEBOOTER	W01	1940	" "
MARAUDER	W98	1938	" "

Length 175′ **Beam** 34′ **Draught** 17′ **Displacement** 1190 tons loaded **Speed** 15 Knots **Engines** Steam triple expansion. Oil fired. 2 boilers. **Fuel** FFO 390 tons **IHP** 3000 **Propulsion** Twin screws. Single Rudder. **Bollard Pull** 30 tons **Complement** RN manned 43. Yardcraft Personnel 30.

HMS Buccaneer (1938)—with battle practice target alongside.

Notes

Designed as Fleet tugs and fitted for firefighting, salvage, rescue and target towing duties. The battle practice targets towed were large and heavy, and needed large tugs fitted with towing winches to handle them.

BANDIT RN manned. 1939 on Fleet Target Service with Home Fleet. 1947 renamed BRITON 13.6.47 arrived Simonstown to relieve SAINT DOGMAEL on target towing duties etc. 17.10.56 with BDO Plymouth and transferred to AS Devonport. 1958 in reserve at Pembroke Dock. 20.4.60 sold to Jos de Smedt, Antwerp.

BRIGAND Based Malta. RN manned. 12.4.60 Paid off after 22 years service in the Mediterranean. 23.9.60 sold to Centieri Navali, Santa Maria, Genoa.

BUCCANEER. RN manned. 1939 on Fleet Target Service with the Home Fleet. 25.8.46 sunk by shell during target practice.

FREEBOOTER RN manned. 1947 at Bermuda relieving RESTIVE. 18.7.49 completed refit at Devonport and transferred to CD. Manned by Yardcraft personnel and based Devonport. 15.6.53 at Coronation Review, Portsmouth. 10.12.59 sold to Centieri Navali, Santa Maria, Genoa.

MARAUDER. RN manned. Based Malta. 20.10.58 sold to Messrs Collins, Submarine Pipe Line Ltd and renamed EMERSON K.

HMS Brigand (1947)

TRUNNION CLASS

Ship	Comp Date	Builder
TAMPEON	1938	Yarwood & Sons, Northwich
TRUNNION	1938	" "

Length 96′ 4″ **Beam** 22′ **Draught** 9′ 6″ **GRT** 177.97 **Speed** 9.5 knots **Engines** Steam triple expansion. Coal fired—45 tons **IHP** 450 **Propulsion** Single screw **Range** 810 miles **Complement** 3 officers 6 ratings.

Notes
TAMPEON Based RNAD, Upnor, Chatham, 9.4.58 transferred to RNAD, Priddys Hard. 13.2.64 sold to Messrs Van Den Bosche & Co, Antwerp. 17.2.64 towed from Portsmouth.
TRUNNION Based RNAD, Bull Point, Plymouth. 12.12.63 sold to H G Pounds, Portsmouth.

ASSURANCE CLASS
All built by Cochrane & Sons Ltd, Selby, Yorkshire.

Ship	Pennant Number	Comp Date
ADEPT	W107	1941
ADHERENT	W108	1941
ALLEGIANCE	W50	1943
ANT (ANTIC)	W141 (A141)	1943
ASSIDUOUS	W142	1943
ASSURANCE	W59	1940
CHARON (ALLIGATOR)	W109	1941

DECISION (HENGIST)	W110 (A110)	1941
DEXTEROUS (ZURMAND)	W111	1942
DILIGENT (TENACITY) (ADHERENT)	W18	1940
EARNEST (EARNER)	W143 (A209)	1943
FRISKY	W11	1941
GRIPER	W112	1942
JAUNTY	W30 (A140)	1941
PROSPEROUS	W96 (A254)	1942
PRUDENT (CAUTIOUS)	W73 (A385)	1940
RESCUE (HORSA)	W97	1942
RESTIVE	W39 (A286)	1940
SAUCY	W131 (A386)	1942
SESAME	W144	1943
STORMCOCK (STORMKING) (TRYPHON)	W87	1942

Length 156′ 6″ **Beam** 35′ **Draught** 16′ 6″ **GRT** 630 tons **Speed** 13 knots **Engines** Steam triple expansion **IHP** 1350 **Fuel** FFO 250 tons **Propulsion** single screw **Bollard Pull** approx 13.5 tons.

Notes

ADEPT 17.3.42 wrecked in the Hebrides.
ADHERENT 14.1.44 foundered in North Atlantic.
ALLEGIANCE On charter to Whampoa Dockyard Co, Hong Kong, 1.7.54. Missing in typhoon and search abandoned 31.8.62.
ANTIC 1943-45 on loan to Royal Netherlands Navy. 26.1.48 commissioned with RN crew as tender to HMS EXCELLENT. 1956 transferred to CD Portsmouth. 1959 to Portland thence Rosyth. 12.11.69 sold to Hughes Bolckow Ltd, Blyth for breaking up. 14.11.69 towed away from Rosyth by tug IRONSIDER.

ASSIDUOUS 1947 at Trincomalee RN manned under C in CEI. 1953 at Gibraltar under CD. 1958 relieved by DEXTEROUS. 10.9.58 sold to H G Pounds, Portsmouth.
ASSURANCE 18.10.41 wrecked in Lough Foyle.
CHARON renamed ALLIGATOR—1949 Naval manned. 1954-58 served at Portsmouth and Portland. July 58 sold to H G Pounds, Portsmouth.
DECISION renamed HENGIST. 1947 RN manned. Based Trincomalee under C in CEI. 1954 at Pembroke Dock in reserve. 15.7.54 sold to D Arnold, Feltham Road, Ashford, Middlesex.
DEXTEROUS 1945 to commercial use, 1957 name changed to ZURMAND.
DILIGENT renamed TENACITY and in 1947 became ADHERENT. Based Sheerness. Relieved CRACKER. 1960 to commercial service as HERMES.

HM Tug Antic (1943)

26

HM Tug Stormking (1943)

EARNEST renamed EARNER RN manned until about 1950 then civilian manned under RFA conditions. 18.1.65 sold to Tsavliris (Salvage and Towage) Ltd, Piraeus, Greece. Renamed NISOS RODOS.

FRISKY 1948 sold to Kuwait Oil Co and renamed HASAN. 1950 renamed VERNICOS MARINA.

GRIPER 1946 to commercial use. 1962 name changed to SURABAJA.

JAUNTY 1949 civilian manned under RFA conditions. 1956-58 based Chatham Yardcraft and PAS manned. 1958 in reserve at Pembroke Dock. 28.8.63 Replaced RESTIVE at Portland for target towing. 19.3.64 at Chatham. 15.11.65 sold to Joseph de Smedt, Antwerp.

PROSPEROUS 1949 Based Portsmouth civilian manned under RFA conditions. 12.5.61 at Chatham in reserve. 7.1.65 sold to Aegean Steam Navigation Co, Piraeus, Greece.

PRUDENT renamed CAUTIOUS. 1949 civilian manned under RFA conditions.13.10.64 sold to Mr Cliff, Tug Boat Co Ltd, Vancouver, Brit. Columbia. Renamed RIVTOW LION.

RESCUE renamed HORSA 16.3.43 Wrecked on Osfles Rock on the East Coast of Iceland.

RESTIVE 8.4.47 RN manned at Bermuda. 28.7.48 paid off at Portland. Transferred to CD Portsmouth. 11.10.54 based Portland on target towing duties. 18.11.64 sailed to Pembroke Dock, destored and de-equipped. 11.6.65 sold to Branco Salvage Ltd, Famagusta, Cyprus. Renamed VENTURA.

SAUCY 1949 civilian manned under RFA conditions. Based Portsmouth/Portland target and coastal towing. 11.11.60 in operational reserve at Pembroke Dock. 1965 sold to Tsavliris (Salvage and Towage) Ltd, Piraeus, Greece. Renamed NISOS CHIOS.

SESAME 11.6.44 sunk by torpedo from E boat off Normandy.

STORMCOCK renamed STORMKING became TRYPHON in 1947. October 1958 sold for commercial use at Sheerness. Renamed MELANIE FAIR.

HM Tug Hengist

HM Tug Restive (1951)

FLAMER CLASS

Ship	Pennant Number	Completion Date	Builder
DRIVER	W100	1943	Alexander Hall, Aberdeen
ENERGY	W101	1943	Alexander Hall, Aberdeen
FLAMER	W31	1940	Alexander Hall, Aberdeen
FRESCO (HANDMAID)	W79	1940	Alexander Hall, Aberdeen
IMPETUS	W60	1940	Alexander Hall, Aberdeen

Length 98′ **Beam** 29′ 2″ **Draught** 14′ **GRT** 233.8 tons **Speed** 10 knots **Engines** Steam reciprocating—coal fired—coal 60 tons **IHP** 850 **Propulsion** Single screw.

Notes
DRIVER Based Rosyth under CD. 26.9.49 at Gibraltar. 27.8.64 sold to Messrs Ditta Carmello Picciotto Fuguis, Messina Sicily.
ENERGY Based Rosyth under CD. January 1946 on loan to Devonport Dockyard. 27.3.46 released from Devonport and arrived Rosyth 3.4.46. 18.12.64 sold to Aegean Steam Navigation, Typalelos Bros Ltd, Piraeus, Greece. Renamed ENERGIA.
FLAMER Based Rosyth under CD. 27.8.65 sold to Tsavliris Shipping Ltd, Piraeus, Greece. 9.9.65 towed away from Rosyth.
FRESCO renamed HANDMAID Based Rosyth under CD. 10.7.70 sold to P W Mackeller Ltd for breaking up. 16.7.70 towed away from Rosyth.
IMPETUS Based Rosyth under CD. 25.4.67 sold to Messrs James A White Ltd, Dunfermline. 8.71 broken up at St Davids, Firth of Forth.

HM Tug Handmaid

MINION CLASS

Ship	Comp Date	Builder
BOMBSHELL	1945	Philip & Son Ltd, Dartmouth
CHAINSHOT	1945	" "
GRAPESHOT	1945	" "
MINION	1940	" "
ROUNDSHOT	·1945	" "

Length 67′, 71′ 6″ OA **Beam** 19′ **Draught** 8′ 6″ **GRT** 56.41 **Speed** 8 knots **Engines** Diesel **Fuel** 7 tons **BHP** 350 **Propulsion** Single screw **Range** 810 miles **Complement** 2 officers, 5 ratings.

HM Tug Roundshot (1945)

32

HM Tug Chainshot

Notes

BOMBSHELL Based Bull Point RNAD Plymouth. 1964 in reserve. 1967 towed to Clyde for further service at Coulport. 1.72 sold to Cabotaje Universal SA Panama for further trading. In service with Polderman Hansweent, Holland; same name (1985).

CHAINSHOT Based at RNAD Priddys Hard, Portsmouth. 4.9.46 Based at RNAD Upnor, Chatham. 18.12.68 Based at RNAD Clyde. 12.3.73 for disposal and sold in running order to Tsavliris Shipping Ltd Greece, renamed AEOLUS.

GRAPESHOT Based RNAD Upnor, Chatham. 5.3.74 sold to Loucas Matsas & Sons, Shipping Co Ltd, Piraeus, Greece. 22.3.74 towed away by tug KELVEDON. 29.6.74 towed to Greece.

MINION Based at RNAD Priddys Hard, Portsmouth. 19.8.60 sold to H G Pounds, Portsmouth.

ROUNDSHOT Based at RNAD Singapore after steaming from UK escorting MFVs to Cochin. 25.9.45 sailed UK for Gibraltar. 8.10.45 sailed Gibraltar for Malta. 26.10.45 sailed Malta for Port Said. 15.11.45 arrived Massawa. 26.12.45 sailed from Aden via Cochin to Penang. February 1946 sailed Penang for Singapore. 5.6.69 sold to Siong Huat, Singapore.

ALLIGATOR CLASS

Ship	Pennant Number	Completion Date	Builder
ALLIGATOR	W51	1941	R Dunston, Hessle
CROCODILE	W88	1941	" "

Length 116′ 9″ **Beam** 26′ 6″ **Draught** 13′ **Displacement** 395 tons **Speed** 12 knots **Engines** Steam triple expansion. Coal fired. **IHP** 1000 **Propulsion** Twin Screws.

Notes
Based in Ceylon under C in CEI.
ALLIGATOR lost in East Indies February/March 1945.
CROCODILE wrecked on SW Coast of India 3.5.46. Salvaged and sold January 1947.

EMPIRE CLASS

All the EMPIRE tugs were of traditional single screw steam tug design similar to previous tugs such as the WARRIOR class. There were however variations in size and power to cover a variety of roles. Built between 1941 and 1946 all had steam triple expansion engines—some were coal fired others oil fired. Many of them undertook very long voyages and gave excellent service from bases world wide. Approximately 144 were built of which the following (about half) were in naval service:-

Ship	Comp Date	Builder
EMPIRE ACE	1942	Cochrane & Sons Ltd, Selby
EMPIRE ANN	1943	A Hall & Co Ltd, Aberdeen
EMPIRE ARIEL	1942	R Dunston Ltd, Thorne
EMPIRE BARBARA	1945	Cochrane & Sons Ltd, Selby
EMPIRE BELLE	1944	J Crown & Sons Ltd, Sunderland

Ship	Comp Date	Builder
EMPIRE BEN (EMPIRE NICHOLSON)	1943	J S Watson Ltd, Gainsborough
EMPIRE CEDAR	1941	R Dunston Ltd, Thorne
EMPIRE CHARLES	1944	H Scarr Ltd, Hessle
EMPIRE CHRISTOPHER	1944	Cochrane & Sons Ltd, Selby
EMPIRE CONNIE	1945	A Hall & Co Ltd, Aberdeen
EMPIRE CUPID	1942	Scott & Sons, Bowling
EMPIRE DARBY	1943	Cochrane & Sons Ltd, Selby
EMPIRE DEMON	1943	Scott & Sons, Bowling
EMPIRE DENIS	1943	Cochrane & Sons Ltd, Selby
EMPIRE DORIS	1944	Scott & Sons, Bowling
EMPIRE DOROTHY	1945	Cook, Welton & Gemmell
EMPIRE FAIRY	1942	Cochrane & Sons Ltd, Selby
EMPIRE FARM	1942	Scott & Sons, Bowling
EMPIRE FRED	1942	A Hall & Co Ltd, Aberdeen
EMPIRE FRIEDA	1946	Fleming & Ferguson Ltd, Paisley
EMPIRE GNOME	1942	A Hall & Co Ltd, Aberdeen
EMPIRE GRIFFIN	1943	Scott & Sons, Bowling
EMPIRE HARLEQUIN	1943	A Hall & Co Ltd, Aberdeen
EMPIRE HUMPHREY	1944	Cochrane & Sons Ltd, Selby
EMPIRE IMP	1942	R Dunston Ltd, Thorne
EMPIRE IVY	1942	Goole S B & Rep Co Ltd
EMPIRE JANE	1944	A Hall & Co Ltd, Aberdeen

Ship	Comp Date	Builder
EMPIRE JENNY	1945	Cochrane & Sons Ltd, Selby
EMPIRE JOAN	1943	" "
EMPIRE JOHN	1943	Clelands (Successors) Ltd, Willington
EMPIRE JONATHAN	1944	A Hall & Co Ltd, Aberdeen
EMPIRE JOSEPHINE	1944	Cochrane & Sons Ltd, Selby
EMPIRE KATY	1945	Goole S B & Rep Co, Ltd
EMPIRE LARCH	1941	" "
EMPIRE LAWN	1942	Ferguson Bros Ltd, Glasgow
EMPIRE LINDEN	1942	R Dunston Ltd, Thorne
EMPIRE LOLA	1946	G Brown & Co Ltd, Greenock
EMPIRE LUCY	1946	J S Watson Ltd, Gainsborough
EMPIRE MADGE	1945	Scott & Sons, Bowling
EMPIRE MASCOT	1943	R Dunston Ltd, Thorne
EMPIRE MEAD	1942	Ferguson Bros Ltd, Glasgow
EMPIRE MINNOW	1943	Scott & Sons, Bowling
EMPIRE MINOTAUR	1942	A Hall & Co Ltd, Aberdeen
EMPIRE NED (EMPIRE EDWARD)	1942	A Hall & Co Ltd, Aberdeen
EMPIRE NETTA	1945	Fleming & Ferguson Ltd
EMPIRE NICHOLAS	1944	J Crown & Sons Ltd, Sunderland
EMPIRE OBERON	1943	R Dunston Ltd, Thorne
EMPIRE PAT	1942	Cochrane & Sons Ltd, Selby
EMPIRE PEGGY	1945	Cook, Welton & Gemmell

Ship	Comp Date	Builder
EMPIRE PHYLLIS	1945	J Crown & Sons Ltd, Sunderland
EMPIRE PIERROT	1943	A Hall & Co Ltd, Aberdeen
EMPIRE PIPER	1942	Clelands (Successors) Ltd, Wilington
EMPIRE PLANE	1941	R Dunston Ltd, Thorne
EMPIRE RACE	1942	" "
EMPIRE RITA	1946	Ferguson Bros Ltd, Glasgow
EMPIRE RODERICK	1946	A Hall & Co Ltd, Aberdeen
EMPIRE ROGER	1944	" "
EMPIRE ROSA	1946	Blyth S B & D D Co Ltd
EMPIRE RUTH	1945	Scott & Sons, Bowling
EMPIRE SAM	1942	Cochrane & Sons Ltd, Selby
EMPIRE SAMSON	1943	Goole S B & Rep Co Ltd
EMPIRE SERAPH	1942	R Dunston Ltd, Thorne
EMPIRE SHIRLEY	1945	A Hall & Co Ltd, Aberdeen
EMPIRE SOPHY	1944	Goole S B & Rep Co Ltd
EMPIRE SPITFIRE	1943	A Hall & Co Ltd, Aberdeen
EMPIRE SPRUCE	1942	R Dunston Ltd, Thorne
EMPIRE TEAK	1942	" "
EMPIRE TESSA	1946	W Simons
EMPIRE TITAN	1942	R Dunston Ltd, Thorne
EMPIRE TITANIA	1943	Scott & Sons, Bowling
EMPIRE VINCENT	1944	Cochrane & Sons Ltd, Selby
EMPIRE WILLOW	1941	R Dunston Ltd, Thorne
EMPIRE ZONA	1946	Fleming & Ferguson Ltd, Paisley

Notes

EMPIRE ACE (DILIGENT) Length 111' 6" OA **Beam** 27' 9"
Draught 11' 6" **GRT** 274.35 **Engines** by Amos & Smith **IHP** 850
Fuel FFO 88 tons **Range** 2640 miles. 7.8.43 to Naval service. 5.3.46
at Malta civilian manned under CD. 29.8.47 renamed DILIGENT.
18.9.58 towed from Malta (for Devonport) by SAUCY. July 1960
towed to Pembroke Dock and reserve. January 1961 Completed
refit at Rosyth and then civilian manned under RFA conditions.
Based on the Clyde. 27.4.61 reverted to original name EMPIRE
ACE. 11.11.68 grounded on Mull of Kintyre. June 1969 salvaged by
RMAS MANDARIN & MFV 64 but beyond economical repair.
19.9.69 sold to A Hood & Co. Broken up at Campbeltown.

EMPIRE ANN (SOLWAY) Length 105' **Beam** 30' **Draught** 12' **GRT**
258. **Engines** by A Hall, **IHP** 1000. Allocated to Malta Dockyard.
11.4.46 for disposal. May 1946 required at Genoa. 29.5.51 sold.
Renamed SOLWAY. March 1977 broken up.

EMPIRE ARIEL (VELOX) Length 95' **Beam** 20' 6" **IHP** 495. On
naval service—under commercial management. Based Ramsey,
Isle of Man and Pembroke Dock under C in C Plymouth. 4.7.47
returned to Overseas Towage and Salvage Co for sale to French
buyers. 24.7.47 sold. renamed VELOX.

HM Tug Empire Ace

38

HM Tug Empire Barbara (at Trinomalee)

EMPIRE BARBARA (ADEPT) Length 105' 9" **Beam** 31' 1"
Draught 11' 6" **GRT** 258 **Engines** Amos & Smith **IHP** 850. Oil
fired. Allocated to C in CEI and sailed for Trincomalee 17.2.45.
Locally manned under Captain Superintendent. 29.8.47 renamed
ADEPT. 1957 sold to Ceylon Government and renamed ALIYA.
1978 sold to Steel Corporation of Sri Lanka for scrap.

EMPIRE BELLE (ELF) Length 105' 9" **Beam** 30' **Draught** 11' 6"
GRT 257 **IHP** 1000. Oil fired. Allocated to C in CEI and sailed to
Bombay 2.8.45. Operated at Bombay with locally entered crew.
Later transferred to Singapore. 29.8.47 renamed ELF at
Singapore. 11.4.60 sold to Augusta Imprise Maritime SPA,
Palermo and renamed MARE JONIO.

EMPIRE BEN Length 106' 6" **Beam** 26' 6" **Draught** 12' **GRT** 243
Engines Clark, IHP 1000 1944 Based Sheerness. 1947 sold. 1948
Renamed EMPIRE NICHOLSON.

EMPIRE CEDAR Length 95' **Beam** 20' 6" **GRT** 129 **IHP** 500. Coal
fired. Allocated to Harwich for harbour towage. 1947 Sold and
renamed HANDYMAN. March 1966 scrapped.

EMPIRE CHARLES (FORTITUDE) Length 105' 9" **Beam** 30' 1"
Draught 12' 4" **GRT** 258 **Engines** by C D Holmes **IHP** 1000 Coal
fired-80 tons. **Speed** 12 knots, **Range** 1900 miles. Allocated to
Portsmouth Dockyard. 29.8.47 renamed FORTITUDE. Civilian
manned. 1962 sold to D Arnold, Feltham Road, Ashford. 1964 sold
to Soc EsercioRimorchie, Salvataggi and renamed FORTITUDO.

EMPIRE CHRISTOPHER Length 107' **Beam** 30' **GRT** 260 **IHP**
1000. On naval service at Rangoon and Singapore. 21.4.46 blew up
and sank at Maungmagon Bay probably mined.

EMPIRE CONNIE Oil fired. Length 105' **Beam** 27' **GRT** 232 **IHP**
900. Sailed to Bombay thence Singapore. 30.6.46 transferred to
Medan and sold to Royal Netherlands Navy and renamed MIES.
Later renamed TELUK AMBON and became harbour tug at
Tandjung Priok, Jakarta, Java.

EMPIRE CUPID (INTEGRITY) Length 113' **Beam** 26' 1" **Draught**
12' 6" **GRT** 259.99 **IHP** 1000. Coal fired 120 tons. **Speed** 12 knots.
Range 1900 miles. Based Greenock. April 1946 reallocated to
Sheerness. 29.8.47 renamed INTEGRITY. 19.5.58 transferred to
Portland. 6.10.61 arrived Pembroke Dock under tow and placed in
reserve. April 1964 sailed Pembroke Dock to Rosyth via
Portsmouth. 30.11.65 sold to Thomas Ward Ltd, Albion Works,
Sheffield for scrap.

EMPIRE DARBY (EGERTON) Length 95' **Beam** 20' 6" **GRT** 130
IHP 675. Based Chatham. 29.8.47 renamed EGERTON. 29.7.58
sold to H G Pounds, Portsmouth.

EMPIRE DEMON Length 113' **Beam** 27' 6" **Draught** 12' **GRT**
259.9 **IHP** 1000. Coal fired 145 tons. Allocated to NOIC Londonderry. Civilian manned under RFA conditions. 14.7.65 for disposal. Sold to Haulbowline Industries Ltd, Co Cork, Ireland.
Broken up at Dublin March 1966.

EMPIRE DENIS Length 107' **Beam** 30' **Draught** 12' **IHP** 1000.
Allocated to C in C Med and operated with Italian crew at Naples.
6.46 released from naval service. 27.8.46 handed over to Messrs
Demattos and Sullivan for C & M pending towage to UK. Sold and
in 1948 was renamed FLYING METEOR. 1963 renamed ROYAL
ROSE and later in 1963 renamed YEWGARTH. 1965 scrapped.

EMPIRE DORIS Length 105' 9" **Beam** 30' 1" **Draught** 12' 4" **GRT**
258 **IHP** 1000. Allocated to C in CEI Persian Gulf December 1945
released from naval service and to British Tanker Co. 1948

HM Tug Fortitude (1951)

renamed BAHRAMᴀND. 1968 sold by B.T.Co to A Shallis & Partners, Iran and renamed TAHAMTAN.

EMPIRE DOROTHY Length 105' 9" **Beam** 30' **Draught** 12' **IHP** 1000. Oil fired. **GRT** 260. 14.10.45 sailed for Far East via Bombay & Singapore. December 1945 arrived Japan. 12.3.46 at Port Swettenham in service of Harbour Board. 17.3.47 sold to Crown Agents. 1958 renamed DOROTHY & in 1976 STRAITS WINNER. 1982 scrapped.

EMPIRE FAIRY Length 107' **Beam** 30' **GRT** 277 **Engines** by Amos & Smith **IHP** 1000. December 1944 allocated to C in CEI at Mombasa. December 1945 at Rangoon and released from naval service. 29.12.45 sold to Rangoon Port Authority. 1946 renamed NATHAMEE.

EMPIRE FARM Length 107' **Beam** 30' **IHP** 1000 **GRT** 260. Based Milford Haven for Reserve Fleet work. 20.11.46 sold and handed over to Wilson & Sons Ltd and renamed LADY ROSEMARY.

EMPIRE FRED Length 105' 2" **Beam** 27' 1"**Draught** 11' 7" **GRT** 233.24 **IHP** 900. Oil fired. **Speed** 10 knots. On naval service at Trieste with Allied Military Government. 30.10.54 arrived Malta towed by EMPIRE EDWARD. 2.7.55 arrived Londonderry towed by SAUCY. Allocated to SNONI civilian manned under RFA conditions. 10.1.66 tug services discontinued at Londonderry but moved to Clyde area. 5.6.70 towed to Chatham (by BUSTLER) and used as an accommodation vessel. 2.10.73 sold in running order and sailed for Holland.

EMPIRE FRIEDA (ORIANA) Length 116' **Beam** 27' 6" **IHP** 800. 1947 based Chatham replaced WEST HYDE. May 1947 renamed ORIANA. 19.1.48 Blew up and sank presumably mined, off Knoll Buoy, Essex Coast whilst towing an MMS to Brightlingsea.

EMPIRE GNOME Length 105' **Beam** 27' **GRT** 233 **IHP** 900. Coal fired. Based Trincomalee. Locally entered civilian crew under Captain Superintendent. 31.7.48 sold and renamed JACOBA.

EMPIRE GRIFFIN Length 105' 6" **Beam** 30' **GRT** 257 **IHP** 1000. 10.6.43 on naval service. 1946 sold September and renamed FORTUNATE.

EMPIRE HARLEQUIN Length 105' **Beam** 27' **GRT** 232 **IHP** 900. Based Alexandria on dockyard duties. Locally manned. July 1946 sold to Sudan Railways and renamed EL GADIR.

EMPIRE HUMPHREY Length 111' 9" oa **Beam** 26' 7" **Draught** 11' 6" **GRT** 258. **Engines** by Amos and Smith **IHP** 1000. August 1945 sailed to Bombay. December 1945 in Batavia under NOIC locally entered Dutch crew employed on harbour service. sold to Dutch authority, renamed SUUS.

EMPIRE IMP Length 102' 9" oa **Beam** 20' 6" **GRT** 130 **IHP** 500. On naval service under commercial management. Harwich—Ostend —Dover—Calais area. November 1947 on dockyard service Sheerness/Chatham. 30.10.59 for disposal at Devonport. August 1960 sold to H G Pounds. 1962 renamed IRVING WALNUT.

EMPIRE IVY Length 107' **Beam** 26' **GRT** 263 **Engines** by C D Holmes **IHP** 1000. Based Clyde. 1946 sold to Clyde Shipping Co Ltd renamed FLYING TEMPEST. 1962 sold to Rimorchiatori Sardi, Italy, renamed POCTTO. 1968 sold to Soc Salvataggi SA Italy, renamed MONTELUNGO.

EMPIRE JANE Length 105' 9" **Beam** 30' 1' **Draught** 12' 4" **GRT** 258 Oil fired. **IHP** 850. August 1945 sailed for Bombay allocated to C in CEI thence to Singapore. March 1947 for disposal. Sold to Union SS Co, New Zealand and renamed TAIOMA.

EMPIRE JENNY (AID) Length 105' **Beam** 30' 1" **Draught** 11' 6" **GRT** 258 **Engines** by Amos and Smith **IHP** 850. **Speed** 10 knots **Range** 2640 miles. Oil fired. Allocated to Trincomalee under Captain Superintendent. UK Master, locally entered crew. 29.8.47 renamed AID. 1952 transferred to Malta and placed in reserve. 1958 transferred to Portsmouth. 26.7.60 for disposal and sold to H G Pounds, Portsmouth who resold her to J D Irving, St John, Canada. Renamed IRVING TEAK.

EMPIRE JOAN (EMPHATIC) Length 95' **Beam** 20' 6" **GRT** 130 **IHP** 650 Coal Fired. On service at Dover. 4.7.46 at Chatham under CD. 29.8.47 renamed EMPHATIC. January 1958 reported unseaworthy and replaced by PROMPT from Malta. 23.7.58 sold to Edmund Hancock (1929) Ltd, Cardiff. 1960 taken over by Bristol Channel Towage Co Ltd. 30.6.63 taken over by R & J Rea Ltd and renamed HALLGARTH. 1966 sold to John Cashmore for demolition.

EMPIRE JOHN Length 135' **Beam** 30' **GRT** 479 **IHP** 1275, oil fired. 4.10.43 Coastal towing duties. 22.2.45 towed TID 2 to Boulogne. Sold. November 1965 broken up in Spain.

EMPIRE JONATHAN (FIDGET) Length 112' 9" **Beam** 27' 6" **Draught** 11' 6" **GRT** 232.28 **IHP** 850 oil fired 71 tons **Range** 1720 miles. 9.7.45 sailed for Bombay. 18.10.45 on station. December 1945 at Singapore under CD. August 1947 renamed FIDGET. 16.6.71 transferred to Singapore Government.

EMPIRE JOSEPHINE Length 107' **Beam** 30' **Draught** 12' **GRT** 274 **IHP** 1000 Oil fired. 6.2.45 allocated to BPF Sydney. April 1946 at Hong Kong on naval service. 17.5.46 paid off and returned to MOT Hong Kong. Transferred to Colonial Government and operated as Police cruising launch.

EMPIRE KATY Length 107' **Beam** 30' **Draught** 12' **GRT** 261 **IHP** 1000 18.10.45 at Bombay. December 1945 at Aden. January 1946 on charter to Aden Port Trust. 23.12.46 sold to Aden Port Trust.

EMPIRE LARCH Length 135' **Beam** 30' **Draught** 12' **GRT** 482 **IHP** 1275. On naval service Cherbourg, Antwerp, Scapa Flow & Leith. 30.12.46 sold to United Towing Co, Hull. Renamed MASTERMAN. 1962 sold and renamed SMJELI

EMPIRE LAWN (MASTERFUL) Length 115' 9" **Beam** 28' 9" **Draught** 12' **GRT** 254 **IHP** 900. Coal fired 108 tons. **Range** 1356 miles. 5.3.46 at Devonport Dockyard under CD. March 1947 renamed MASTERFUL. 19.9.58 sold and renamed SANANTONIO PRIMO. 1981 scrapped.

EMPIRE LINDEN Length 107' **Beam** 30' **Draught** 12' **GRT** 245 **IHP** 1000. **Engines** by C D Holmes. December 1944 allocated to C in CEI at Kilindini. Released from naval service and handed over to Kenya and Uganda Harbour and Railway Co. December 1945 on loan to British Tanker Co, Bandar Mashur. 26.3.48 sold to Tanganyika Railways.

EMPIRE LOLA (JUSTICE) Length 116' **Beam** 27' 6" **GRT** 300. **Engines** by Rankin & Blackmore **IHP** 800. June 1947 at Bermuda to replace SAINT BLAZEY. 29.8.47 renamed JUSTICE. On dockyard service under Captain Superintendent and Master Attendant. 24.3.51 transferred to Bermuda Government. 21.7.67 sunk as a target off Bermuda.

EMPIRE LUCY Length 118' 6" **Beam** 27' **GRT** 243.87. **Engines** by G Fletcher & Co. **IHP** 1000. Oil fired. 1946-58 allocated to Harwich. 1962 sold to Imprese Maritime, SpA, Italy and renamed OGNINA.

EMPIRE MADGE (WEASEL) Length 114' **Beam** 31' 4" **Draught** 12' 4" **GRT** 258 **IHP** 1000. Oil fired—98.36 tons. **Range** 2020 miles. 12.7.45 arrived Port Said, 8.10.45 Bombay. December 1945 at Singapore on naval service with locally entered crew. UK officers. 29.8.48 renamed WEASEL. 8.11.68 sold as a runner to Hong Huat Hardware Co Ltd. Singapore for further trading.

EMPIRE MASCOT Length 106' 6" **Beam** 26' 6" **GRT** 244 **Engines** by C D Holmes **IHP** 1000. 19.5.43 on naval service. 27.7.46 sold. 1947 renamed METINDA IV. 1949 renamed FLYING KESTREL. 1969 scrapped.

EMPIRE MEAD Length 105' 2" **Beam** 27' **Draught** 11' 7" **GRT** 232.28. Coal fired. **IHP** 900. December 1945 at Singapore on naval service with locally entered crew. 2.9.47 for disposal and sold locally. Renamed BODEKER.

EMPIRE MINNOW Length 107' **Beam** 30' **GRT** 258 **IHP** 1000. Oil fired. 1946 on naval service at Venice. 1.7.48 sold to British India Steam Navigation Co Ltd. Renamed THIKA.

EMPIRE MINOTAUR Length 105' **Beam** 27' **GRT** 233 Coal fired **IHP** 900. 1945 operating under Captain Superintendent Trincomalee with locally entered crew. 1949 sold to Townsville Harbour Board, Australia. Renamed LALOR. Believed scuttled in 1969.

EMPIRE NED Length 105' 2" **Beam** 27' 2" **Draught** 11' 7" **GRT** 233.6 **IHP** 900 Oil fired 78 tons. March 1943 renamed EMPIRE EDWARD. On naval service at Trieste with Allied Military Government. 30.10.54 arrived Malta towing EMPIRE FRED. April 1955 both tugs towed to UK. 19.5.55 allocated to Chatham Dockyard. 31.10.55 Renamed ENERGETIC. 9.5.65 sold to Tsavliris (Salvage and Towing) Ltd, Piraeus, Greece and renamed NISOS LEFKOS. 1.9.65 left Sheerness (under tow) with SALVIGIL. November 1975 sold to Maritime Commercial Enterprises Ltd, Greece and renamed KRONOS.

EMPIRE NETTA Length 123' 9" **Beam** 29' 3" **Draught** 14' **GRT** 297.05 Oil fired—134 tons. **IHP** 800. Based Milford Haven. Civilian manned under RFA conditions. 17.10.67 sold to Jos de Smedt, Antwerp for breaking up.

EMPIRE NICHOLAS Length 107' **Beam** 30' **GRT** 257 **IHP**1000. December 1945 at Japan. 12.3.46 at Batavia on harbour service under NOIC with locally entered Dutch crew. Sold to a Dutch Authority.

EMPIRE OBERON Length 107' **Beam** 30' **GRT** 242 **IHP**1000. Based at Hong Kong. December 1945 released from naval service and transferred to Rangoon Port Authority. May 1947 laid up at Rangoon, taken over by Mackinnons and sold.

EMPIRE PAT Length 107' **Beam** 30' **GRT** 274 **IHP** 1000. Handed over to British Tanker Co Bandar Mashur.

EMPIRE PEGGY Length 107' **Beam** 30'. **Engines** by C D Holmes. **GRT** 259 **IHP** 1000. 30.8.45 Sailed to Bombay thence Singapore. 16.11.45 arrived Singapore allocated to BRNO Saigon 16.5.46 to French navy at Medan. 19.4.48 returned from French navy. 1949 sold to Queensland Tug Co & renamed CORINGA.

EMPIRE PHYLLIS Length 105' 6" **Beam** 30' **GRT** 306 **IHP** 1000. **Engines** by N E Marine. Allocated to C in CEI for Palk Straight. December 1945 at Trincomalee. 17.2.46 Arrived Bombay and placed in C & M. 20.1.47 sold to Anglo Iranian Oil Co. 1948 renamed HYAT. 1961 renamed BRUCOLI.

EMPIRE PIERROT Length 105' **Beam** 27' **GRT** 232 **IHP** 850. **Engines** by A Hall. Oil fired. Allocated to C in CEI at Mombasa. December 1945 at Singapore. 7.5.47 for disposal. 14.1.48 sold. Renamed ST PATRICK.

EMPIRE PIPER Length 107' **Beam** 30' **GRT** 250 **IHP** 1000. March 1946 with Captain of Dockyard Portsmouth/Portland. 24.7.46 on naval service Marchwood with Risdon Beasley. 12.12.46 released from naval service. Sold to John Cooper (Belfast) Ltd and renamed PIPER. 1971 to Greece as SOTIRIOS.

EMPIRE PLANE Length 92' 6" **Beam** 20' 5" **Draught** 8' 4" **GRT** 129. **Engine** by McKie & Baxter. **IHP** 500. Coal fired. 1947 under RNO Clyde. 8.4.49 transferred to BDO Clyde—civilian manned under RFA conditions. 31.8.53 at Portsmouth for refit and reserve. 5.4.57 for disposal. April 1958 sold and renamed RIVER ESKIMO. 1964 scrapped.

EMPIRE RACE Length 107' **Beam** 30' **GRT** 242 **IHP** 1000. Coal fired. 1946 based Harwich. 1962 sold to Capieci DI Nav and renamed CAPO D'ORLANDO.

HM Tug Frisky

EMPIRE RITA (FRISKY) Length 123′ 9″ OA. **Beam** 29′ 3″ OA.
Draught 9′ 6″ **GRT** 294.83 **IHP** 800. Oil fired—134 tons. Allocated
to RNO Clyde. 11.4.49 transferred to BDO Clyde and civilian
manned under RFA conditions. 11.9.58 at Portsmouth for refit
and transferred to PAS to replace FORTITUDE. 1959 renamed
FRISKY. 1960 transferred to C D Malta. 8.4.63 transferred to
Gibraltar and towed there by BUSTLER. 26.6.70 sold to S O Mar
Ltd. Valletta, Malta. Renamed CREO. 1979 Scrapped.

EMPIRE RODERICK (SECURITY) Length 112′ 9″ **Beam** 27′ 6″
Draught 11′ 6″ **GRT** 233.24 **IHP** 900. Oil fired—78 tons. Allocated
to Captain in Charge Portland. 29.8.47 renamed SECURITY. 1961
at Portsmouth. 12.8.63 at Chatham supplying steam to CALDY.
4.4.66 sold to Jos de Smedt, Antwerp.

EMPIRE ROGER Length 105′ **Beam** 27′ **IHP** 850. Oil fired.
Engines by A Hall. April 1946 at Kure, Japan. May 1946 allocated
to Hong Kong. 11.3.47 on charter to Taikoo Co, Hong Kong. Sold
to Shipping and Freighting Ltd, London. 1958 resold to Sirespa
Building Co Ltd.

47

EMPIRE ROSA Length 116' **Beam** 27' 6" **Draught** 11' **GRT** 292.15. Oil fired—134 tons. 21.7.46 at Scapa Flow to replace EMPIRE TEAK. Civilian manned and managed by Overseas Towage and Salvage Co Ltd. 1948 operated by SORF Pembroke Dock. 2.4.49 transferred to Director of Boom Defence and civilian manned under RFA conditions. 15.10.63 transferred to Clyde and as relief tug for Londonderry. 28.11.70 civilian manned but no longer under RFA conditions and transferred to Invergordon. 29.3.72 used as a target vessel. 3.12.77 broke adrift from her moorings and washed ashore in Luce Bay. Refloated by the salvage vessel RMAS MANDARIN and sold to Arnott Young for breaking up at Troon.

EMPIRE RUTH Length 105' **Beam** 30' **Draught** 12' **GRT** 257.93. **Engines** by Plenty & Sons Ltd, **IHP** 1000. **Speed** 10 knots. Oil fired—90 tons. Allocated to C in CEI at Trincomalee and locally manned. Sold about 1949 renamed HADHIR.

EMPIRE SAM Length 107' **Beam** 30' **GRT** 274 **IHP** 1000. Allocated to C in CEI Colombo. 3.4.45 sailed for Australia. 12.6.45 arrived Darwin. 30.8.45 Sailed for Hong Kong. 18.9.45 arrived Hong Kong. May 1947 operated by Colonial Government as a Police cruising launch.

EMPIRE SAMSON Length 105' 6" **Beam** 30' **GRT** 261. **Engines** by Amos & Smith **IHP** 1000. Coal fired. Allocated to C in CEI at Trincomalee. Not required and sailed to Bombay for C & M. 30.6.47 sold to Government of India. Renamed SAKTI.

EMPIRE SERAPH Length 95' **Beam** 20' 6" **GRT** 129. On naval service at Calais. 3.9.47 sold. Renamed BIZON.

EMPIRE SHIRLEY Length 105' 2" **Beam** 27' **Draught** 11' 7" **GRT** 232.28 **IHP** 850. Allocated to C in CEI. 7.9.45 sailed for Bombay. December 1945 not required by C in CEI and to Singapore. March 1947 for disposal at Singapore. August 1947 sold to Port of Wellington and renamed TAPUHI.

EMPIRE SOPHY (BEHEST) Length 107' **Beam** 30' **Draught** 12' **GRT** 261 **IHP** 1000. Allocated to C in CEI under Captain Superintendent Trincomalee. UK Yardcraft officers and locally entered crew. 29.8.47 renamed BEHEST. About 1950 transferred to Colombo Port Authority and now lies (sunk) in Colombo Harbour.

EMPIRE SPITFIRE (WARDEN) (PROMPT) Length 112' 9" OA. **Beam** 27' 6" **Draught** 12' **GRT** 232.28. **Engines** by A Hall **IHP** 900 Oil fired. Allocated to C D Malta. 29.8.47 renamed WARDEN. 1951 renamed PROMPT. 1957 towed to Chatham. 7.7.75 sold to Thames Services, Tilbury. Renamed TORQUE. Preserved at Maryport Maritime Museum (Cumbria).

EMPIRE SPRUCE (EMULOUS) Length 92' **Beam** 20' 6" **Draught** 10' 6" **GRT** 129 **IHP** 500. Allocated to C D Chatham to relieve either SUNBIRD or SUNFISH. 29.8.47 renamed EMULOUS. 11.47 Basin tug CHATHAM. 23.5.58 sold to H G Pounds, Portsmouth. 1961 sold by Pounds after motorising to J D Irving Ltd, St Johns and renamed IRVING OAK.

EMPIRE TEAK Length 106' 6" **Beam** 26' 6" **GRT** 243 **IHP** 1000. Coal fired. On naval service under commercial management at Scapa Flow and coastal towing. 7.7.47 allocated to Director of Boom Defence Gosport for trials. August 1947 replaced EMPIRE IMP at Harwich with SORF. 23.8.50 sold to Alexandra Towing Co Ltd and removed from Harwich. Renamed BRAMBLES. 1970 scrapped.

EMPIRE TESSA (EMINENT) Length 123' 9" OA **Beam** 29' 3" OA **GRT** 294.83. **Engine** by W Simons **IHP** 800. Allocated to Bermuda. 29.8.47 renamed EMINENT. 18.1.51 seriously damaged by fire in Bermuda. 1951 at Portsmouth Dockyard under CD. 5.2.69 transferred to Clyde. 7.7.75 sold in running order to Medway Maritime Museum. 2.8.75 towed away by tug CERVIA. 1982 Renamed GOLIATH and transferred to Maryport Maritime Museum, Cumbria.

EMPIRE TITAN Length 113' 7" OA **Beam** 26' 7" **Draught** 10' **GRT** 242. **Engine** by C D Holmes **IHP** 1000. Coal fired. 24.3.47 To Lagos with Gold Coast Government.

EMPIRE TITANIA (VAGRANT) Length 114' **Beam** 31' 4" **Draught** 12' **GRT** 257.93. Oil fired—80 tons **IHP** 1000 **Speed** 12 knots. **Range** 1900 miles. 1946 Mediterranean Command at Naples. 1947 allocated to Chatham Dockyard under CD. 29.8.47 renamed VAGRANT. 25.9.59 transferred to Gibraltar. 29.3.68 sold in running order to Mr Carmello Piccioto, Messina. Renamed MARY ELIZABETH.

PAS Resolve

EMPIRE VINCENT Length 107′ **Beam** 30′ **GRT** 274 **IHP** 1000. 11.7.45 sailed Gibraltar for Bombay. 18.10.45 at Bombay. December 1945 on service with RNO Bangkok manned by locally entered crew. 1946 sold to Siam. Renamed SAMAESAN.

EMPIRE WILLOW Length 95′ **Beam** 20′ 6″ **Engines** by McKie & Baxter **GRT** 129 **IHP** 500. 1945 based Bull Point, Plymouth. 1946 sold. Renamed LOS.

EMPIRE ZONA (RESOLVE) Length 123′ 9″ **Beam** 29′ 3″ **GRT** 289.9 **IHP** 850. Oil fired—134 tons. Based Clyde with RNO. 13.5.49 transferred to Director of Boom Defence and civilian manned under RFA conditions. 30.12.57 transferred to Chatham to relieve EGERTON. PAS manned. 25.6.58 renamed RESOLVE. 21.11.69 transferred to Rosyth for a trial period as basin tug. 21.1.71 towed from Rosyth to Chatham. October 1973 for sale at Chatham. 1974 sold to Greece.

Other EMPIRE tugs (not in naval service) were:
EMPIRES AID, ALFRED, ANDREW, ASH, BECKY, BESS, BETSY, BIRCH, BRACKEN, CADET, CHERUB, CLARA, DARLING, DOLLY, ELINOR, FIR, FLORA, FOLK, FRANK, GOBLIN, GRETA, HARRY, HELEN, HENCHMAN, HILDA, JEAN (2), JESTER, JULIA, JUNA, LEONARD, LEWIS, LILLIPUT, MAID, MAISIE, MAPLE, MARTHA, MARY (ex JEAN), MEADOW, MUSTANG, NAN, NINA, NORA, OAK, PALM, PAM, PAUL, PERCY, PINE, PIXIE, POLLY, RAYMOND, RUPERT, SALLY, SANDY, SARA, SHEILA, SILAS, SIMON, SINEW, SPRITE, STELLA, STORMCOCK, SUSAN, SYBIL, THISTLE, TOBY, VERA, WALTER, WARLOCK, WINNIE, WOLD.

BUSTLER CLASS

Ship	Pennant Number	Completion Date	Builder
BUSTLER	W72 (A240)	1942	Henry Robb, Leith
GROWLER (CYCLONE)	W105 (A111)	1943	" "
HESPER (HESPERIA)	W106	1943	" "
MEDIATOR	W125	1944	" "
REWARD	W164 (A264)	1945	" "
SAMSONIA	W23 (A218)	1942	" "
TURMOIL	W169	1945	" "
WARDEN	W170 (A309)	1945	" "

Length 205′ **Beam** 40′ 5″ **Draught** 16′ 11″ **GRT** 1100 **Speed** 16 knots **Engines** Atlas Polar 8 cylinder x 2. **BHP** 3020 **Propulsion** Single screw **Bollard Pull** 30 tons **Range** 5000 miles @ 12 knots.

HMS Bustler

HM Tug Growler (as Welshman)

Notes

The first fleet tugs with diesel engines. Designed for sea towing, salvage and rescue. Not suitable for harbour work.

BUSTLER Used as fleet tug during the war. 1947-58 chartered out for commercial use. Civilian manned from 1959 under RFA conditions. 27.7.73 sold to Brodospas (Yugoslavia) and towed away by Yugoslav tug BORAK on 4.8.73. Renamed MOCNI.

GROWLER Whilst on charter was renamed CAROLINE MOLLER in 1947-1952, CASTLE PEAK in 1954 and WELSHMAN in 1962. 23.10.63 renamed CYCLONE. Civilian manned under RFA conditions. 1977 laid up at Gibraltar. 16.4.83 Sold to Eagle Tugs Ltd, Georgetown, Grand Cayman for use at Mombasa. Removed from Gibraltar and renamed MARTIAL.

HESPER renamed HESPERIA. Lost 9.2.45—wrecked on the coast of Libya.

HMS Reward (1945)

MEDIATOR 1959 at Malta RN manned. 10.5.64 arrived Plymouth for disposal. 26.2.65 sold to Tsavliris (Salvage and Towage) Ltd. Piraeus, Greece and renamed NISOS ZAKYNTHOS. 1975 resold to Maritime Commercial Enterprises Ltd.

REWARD 1949 RN manned. 1957 at Chatham being placed in state of preservation. 1958 transferred to Pembroke Dock reserve. 22.3.60 arrived Malta (towed by AGILE) for Target Squadron. Naval manned by crew of BRIGAND. 22.1.62 sailed for Gibraltar and Chatham. 1.5.62 On charter to United Towing Co as ENGLISH-MAN. 2.6.63 manned under RFA conditions and based Portsmouth. 23.2.71 at Malta with UK officers and local crew. October 1971 returned to Portsmouth. July 1973 in reserve at Pembroke Dock. 20.1.75 arrived Chatham under tow. Taken over by RN as HMS REWARD for patrol duties in offshore oilfields. 10.8.76 sank in Firth of Forth after collision with German freighter PLAINSMAN. 29.8.76 raised by MAGNUS III and sold for scrap to Jas White & Co Ltd, St David's Harbour.

SAMSONIA 1947 on Civil Charter as FOUNDATION JOSEPHINE. 1958 at Portsmouth manned under RFA conditions. 1965 transferred to Devonport. 28.2.74 sold to Brodus Split, Salvage, Towage and Demolition Enterprises, Yugoslavia and towed away after Tyne refit. Renamed JAKI.

TURMOIL Most of early career on charter to civilian tug companies. 1963 to Pembroke Dock for disposal. 15.1.65 sold to Tsavliris (Salvage and Towage) Ltd, Piraeus, Greece for further use. Renamed NISOS KERKYRA later renamed MATSAS.

WARDEN 1946-51 on charter as TWYFORD. 1959 at Portsmouth for refit. Civilian manned under RFA conditions. January 1965 towed by TYPHOON to Pembroke Dock and reserve. 18.11.69 sold to Tsavliris (Salvage and Towage) Ltd, Piraeus, Greece. Renamed NISOS DELOS.

HM Tug Warden

HM Tug Samsonia (1962)

HMS Nimble (1942)

NIMBLE CLASS

Ship	Pennant Number	Completion Date	Builder
CAPABLE	W171 (A508)	1946	Fleming & Ferguson
CAREFUL	W172 (A293)	1946	" "
EXPERT	W173 (A172)	1945	" "
NIMBLE	W123 (A223)	1942	" "

Length 175′ **Beam** 35′ 8″ **Draught** 17′ **GRT** 831.89 **Speed** 15 knots **Engines** Steam triple expansion, 2 boilers **Fuel** FFO 296 tons **IHP** 3000 **Propulsion** Twin screws, single rudder **Bollard Pull** 30 tons **Range** 7000 miles **Complement** 30.

HM Tug Careful (1953)

HM Tug Capable

Notes

Designed for sea towing, salvage and harbour work, and proved to be excellent tugs. Fitted with spring towing hooks but (surprisingly) not fitted with towing winches. Bridges were originally open; wheelhouses were fitted later.

CAPABLE Allocated to C D Portsmouth. 1948 controllable pitch propellers fitted experimentally. 1971 on loan to Portland. 28.9.71 transferred to C D Devonport. 18.7.73 sold to W H Arnott, Young & Co Ltd, Dalmuir, Clyde.

CAREFUL Allocated to C D Devonport. 6.5.65 towed by SAMSONIA to Pembroke Dock. December 1973 sold to Thomas Ward, Albion Works, Sheffield for demolition.

EXPERT Allocated to C D Malta. 30.10.68 sold to Tsavliris (Salvage & Towage) Ltd, Piraeus, Greece. Renamed NISOS MYKONOS.

NIMBLE Allocated to C D Gibraltar to replace SAINT OMAR. 12.7.60 arrived Portsmouth towed by BUSTLER. Refitted at Chatham. May 1962 sailed Chatham for Singapore. 17.7.62 handed over to C D Singapore. 10.4.70 reduced to reserve. 5.6.71 transferred to Singapore Government.

ROCK CLASS
Canadian built between 1943 and 1945

Ship	Pen. Number	Builder
ROCK CLIFF	W15	Midlands Shipyard Co Ltd
ROCK FOREST	W66 (A166)	Canadian S B & Eng Co Ltd, Ontario
ROCK GLEN (FREEDOM)	W26 (A296)	" "
ROCK LAND (FLARE)	W79 (A279)	Midlands Shipyard Co Ltd
ROCK MOUNT	W38 (A138)	" "
ROCK PIGEON (FLAUNT)	W88 (A388)	Canadian S B & Eng Co Ltd, Ontario
ROCK PORT	W52	Midlands Shipyard Co Ltd
ROCK WING	W04 (A233)	" "

Length 105′ **Beam** 30′ **Draught** 12′ 6″ **GRT** 233 **Engines** Steam triple expansion. Oil fired—80 tons. **IHP** 1000 **Propulsion** Single screw **Range** 2000 miles.

Notes

ROCKCLIFF Allocated to BPF Sydney. 7.6.45 sailed Montreal for Sydney via Honolulu, Pago and Suva. 24.8.45 Arrived Sydney. 27.10.45 at Brisbane. April 1946 at Hong Kong. 21.5.46 paid off. August 1947 sold to Taikoo Dockyard and Eng Co Ltd, Hong Kong. Renamed TAIKOO CHEONG.

ROCK FOREST Allocated to BPF Sydney. 8.8.45 sailed Montreal to Habana & San Francisco. April 1946 at Townsville. February 1947 at Hong Kong, naval manned for harbour duties and target towing. 16.7.47 paid off. August 1947 sold to United Overseas Petroleum Co, London and renamed ARAMICO 20.

ROCK GLEN 10.6.45 sailed Montreal for Sydney. May 1946 at Hong Kong—civilian manned on naval service. 29.8.48 renamed FREEDOM. 16.11.54 at Singapore under C D. 8.8.55 at Hong Kong. 17.8.59 at Singapore. 1971 transferred to Singapore Government.

ROCK LAND 4.9.45 sailed Montreal for New York thence to Singapore via Azores. 21.6.46 transferred to Hong Kong. On naval service towing and berthing—civilian manned. 29.8.48 renamed FLARE. 17.10.59 sold to Whampoa Docks.

ROCK MOUNT 11.9.45 sailed Montreal for New York, Panama, Pearl Harbour, Sydney. 27.10.45 arrived Sydney. April 1946 at Townsville. May 1946 allocated to Hong Kong. 2.9.47 for disposal. December 1947 sold to Wilson & Sons Ltd, London and renamed SABRE.

ROCK PIGEON 31.8.45 arrived Montreal from Kingston, Ontario. Sailed to Hong Kong via Singapore. April 1946 at Hong Kong on general towage duties. 12.2.47 Civilian manned on naval service. 29.8.48 renamed FLAUNT. 16.11.54 under C D for towage and ship movements at Singapore. 6.6.55 at Hong Kong. 3.6.69 sold to Falmouth Towage Co. Renamed ST MERRYN. 1984 scrapped.

ROCK PORT 12.8.45 sailed Montreal for New York, Pearl Harbour and arrived Canton Island 10.10.45. April 1946 at Townsville. May 1946 on naval service Hong Kong. August 1947 sold to Overseas Petroleum Co Ltd, London. Renamed TAPLINE I.

ROCK WING With British Pacific Fleet 1945-46 then Hong Kong Dockyard. Sold 1948 renamed TAPLINE 2.

TID CLASS TUGS

The 'TID' class tug was born from the urgent necessity to replace tugs lost through enemy action and to provide vessels suitable to support the impending invasion preparations. The origin of the 'TID' abbreviation remains controversial with interpretations varying from; 'Tug Invasion Duty' to 'Tug Intermediate Design' to 'TIDDLER'.

One hundred and eighty two vessels were built, numbered from TID 1 to 183 but with no number 13. From their inception these small tugs were designed to be built using a minimum of valuable shipyard resources. As an alternative many non-marine welding and fabricating companies were employed, from all over Britain, making the best use possible of spare wartime capacity. The hulls were of hard chine design, to simplify plate moulding, and assembled from seven major welded units. The maximum size of each unit was 10 tons in weight and 10ft in length and governed by the need to transport them individually by road. Assembly was carried out mainly by the Dunston yards at Thorne and Hessle but during the latter stages a small number were constructed by Wm Pickersgill at Sunderland.

A small two cylinder compound type steam engine was used, with steam being supplied by a simple natural draught boiler. The first 90 vessels were coal fired but all subsequent tugs were completed to burn oil fuel. This power plant produced a maximum of 220 indicated horsepower to drive a single, cast iron, screw propeller. Funnels were hinged for folding down. Wheelhouses were not fitted "as built" but were added to some later.

Construction started in 1943 and continued until late 1946. During peak production, new tugs were being turned out at a rate of one vessel every 4½ days.

The entire series of 'TID' class tugs were built to the order of the Ministry of War Transport, with allocations being made for 'Naval Service', to various Army units and to civilian organisations. At the cessation of hostilities a number of tugs were designated for Admiralty use and transferred permanently to Naval Service.

Length BP 65' **Beam** 17' **Depth** 8' **Draught** 6' approx on even keel with ½ bunkers. **Construction** steel, fabricated, all welded. **Gross Tonnage** 54 tons. **Machinery IHP** 220 **RPM** in service—175. Boiler—one natural draught. **Speed** 8½ knots.

The following TIDS have recorded naval service

TID 2   Completed 3.4.43. Allocated to 21 Army Group.
(C677)   22.2.45 towed to Boulogne by EMPIRE JOHN. 6.12.45
         arrived Sheerness and transferred to SNSO for Fleet
         Fuelling Service. 26.4.46 renumbered C677. November
         1958 sold to E Millanger, Montreal. 1961 sold to J D
         Irving, ST Johns and renamed IRVING FIR. Converted
         to diesel.
TID 3   Completed 20.4.43. Allocated to Captain of Dockyard,
         Portsmouth. 11.2.52 transferred to RNAD Upnor,
         Chatham. 20.10. 58 returned to C D Portsmouth (PAS).
         24.8.73 sold to Controlled Thermic Lancing Ltd,
         Barking.

TID 3

TID 4   Completed 28.4.43. MOWT service. 1948 allocated to
         C D Portsmouth. 19.9.58 sold. 1961 resold to J D
         Irving, renamed IRVING PINE and converted to diesel.
TID 5   Completed 10.5.43. MOWT commercial service.
         13.4.44 transferred to War Department. 1947
         transferred to RN Mine Depot, Milford Haven. 1950
         sold to F T Everard Ltd. 1953 renamed E A EVERARD.
         1971 scrapped.

TID 9	Completed 28.6.43. On naval service in the Mediterranean. 1948 transferred to Admiralty from MOWT. 1948 sold to Italy as RICCARDI 2.
TID 10	Completed 28.6.43. On naval service in the Mediterranean. 1948 transferred to Civil Engineer Malta for towing hopper barges. 2.4.56 for disposal. 1960 sold to Baileys Shipyard, Malta.
TID 11	Completed 15.7.43. Allocated to Gibraltar Dockyard. September 1962 replaced by TANAC 83 from Malta. 16.4.63 sold to Captain W J Havens c/o Australia House, London. August 1963 resold to S Bezzina & Son, Malta renamed SABO, 18.6.63 left Gibraltar towed by TID 56—Converted to diesel. 1974 scrapped.
TID 21	Completed 27.9.43. MOWT commercial service. Managed by Great Western Railway. 23.2.44 transferred to U S Army. 10.11.44 at Portland. 6.12.44 returned to MOWT and managed by Channel Dartmouth Coaling Co. 22.7.46 at Portsmouth on harbour service. 5.8.47 at Devonport for refit. 17.1.48 shipped (in SS PACIFIC LIBERTY) to C D Malta. 23.3.59 transferred to Baileys Shipyard, Malta.
TID 23	Completed 18.10.43. allocated to War Department. September 1944 transferred to Naval Service at Portsmouth Dockyard. 10.10.45 transferred to D of ST. 12.10.45 laid up. Chartered to Risdon Beazley Ltd and renamed ASHFORD 23. 1947 sold to Peter Foster and Co Ltd, Hull and renamed TIDSPUR. 1956 sold to United Towing Co Ltd Hull. 28.4.63 scrapped by Hendrik Ido. Ambacht, Holland.
TID 24	Completed 21.10.43. MOWT Naval service. 10.11.44 at Dover 6.2.45 at Ostend under Nore Command. Allocated to Portsmouth Dockyard. RN crew paid off. 10.9.52 to D of ST. Chartered to Risdon Beazley Ltd and renamed ASHFORD 24. 1953 sold to United Towing Co Ltd Hull, renamed BOWMAN. 23.4.63 scrapped by Hendrik Ido. Ambacht, Holland.
TID 25	Completed 27.10.43. MOWT naval service and with US Army. 29.6.46 laid up and sold to Finnish Government. Renamed B3. 1947 sold to commercial concern in Finland. Renamed MOTTI. 1959 scrapped.

TID 27	Completed 15.11.43. Allocated to Portsmouth Command. May 1946 allocated SORF at Pembroke Dock. 12.9.50 re-allocated to SORF, Clyde and towed there by EMPIRE ZONA on 23.10.50. 1.6.52 sold to Dashwood & Partners Ltd.
TID 28	Completed 29.11.43. MOWT naval service. 16.3.45 allocated to Portsmouth. May 1946 at Southampton under Director of Salvage. 7.9.46 to Messrs Tamlyn & Co, Plymouth for C & M. 1949 sold to Hull Steam Trawlers Mutual Insurance and Protecting Co Ltd. Renamed TRIVVE. 1966 scrapped at Newhaven.
TID 29	Completed 29.11.43. MOWT naval service. 10.11.44 with 21 Army Group. 12.12.44 sailed for Dieppe. 16.3.45 allocated to Portsmouth. 27.8.46 laid up under C & M. 1947 sold to United Africa Co Ltd and renamed GEDU.
TID 30	Completed 8.6.43. MOWT coastal operation. September 1944 with US Army. 25.12.44 laid up. 15.1.45 Portsmouth Dockyard list. 12.4.45 to commercial service. 31.1.46 laid up. 1946 sold to Finnish Government. Renamed B4. 1948 sold to Oulu Oy and renamed OULU 12. 1970 scrapped.
TID 32 (C702)	Completed 19.8.43. In War Department Service. September 1944 allocated to Portsmouth. 5.3.45 transferred to Nore Command and sailed to Ostend. 28.2.46 transferred to C in C Plymouth and allocated to SVSO. 11.4.49 transferred to SNSO Devonport for Fleet Fuelling Duties and renumbered C702. 1.4.58 transferred to PAS for disposal. Transferred to Portsmouth. 27.1.67 sold to H G Pounds, Portsmouth.
TID 33	Completed 3.9.43. MOWT commercial service. December 1943 with 21 Army Group. June 1944 sank at Arromanches during gales which followed D-day landings.
TID 35	Completed 20.9.43. MOWT commercial service. December 1943 US Army service. 22.12.44 laid up. 15.1.45 Portsmouth Dockyard. 4.4.45 MOWT Commercial service. 31.1.46 laid up. Sold to Finnish Government. Renamed B5. 1947 sold to commercial concern in Finland, renamed TOMMI.

TID 43	Completed 9.11.43. Allocated to Portsmouth Pool operating in the Portsmouth, Southampton and Shoreham areas. 2.10.46 to Messrs Townsend Bros for disposal. 1949 sold to Foremost Dredging Co Ltd. Renamed TIDEALL. Converted to diesel.
TID 44	Completed 18.11.43. Allocated to Portsmouth Pool. 3.12.44 capsized and sank while assisting an LST at the Hards. 16.3.45 salvaged and reallocated to Portsmouth Pool. 27.8.46 to Messrs Townsend Bros as agents for D of ST for disposal. 1947 sold to Hull Steam Trawlers Mutual Insurance and Protecting Co Ltd. Renamed KIERO. 1964 scrapped Newhaven.
TID 45	Completed 30.11.43. MOWT naval service Portsmouth. 8.10.45 paid off. 10.10.45 to D of ST. December 1952 to War Department, Marchwood.
TID 46	Completed 4.12.43. Allocated to Portsmouth Pool. 16.3.45 commenced service with Trinity House. August 1947 transferred to C in C Plymouth for mooring duties with BDO. 6.12.57 transferred to Captain in Charge, Portland. 9.1.59 sold to Pounds, Portsmouth.
TID 50	Completed 31.12.43. Portsmouth Command and service at Portland. 5.3.46 transferred to C D Portsmouth. 1960 for sale at Portsmouth. 1968 sold to H G Pounds, Portsmouth for scrap.
TID 52	Completed 5.1.44. Portsmouth Command. 16.3.45 Portsmouth Pool. 23.8.47 transferred to C D Chatham for basin duties. 9.9.63 sold to Messrs Lacmots Ltd, Sheerness Harbour Estate.
TID 54	Completed 22.1.44. MOWT naval service at Portsmouth. 29.6.45 laid up then chartered to Westminster Dredging. 1948 sold to River Wear Commissioners. Renamed BIDDICK. 1973 sold for preservation but lying derelict at Point Wharf, River Thames.
TID 56 (C688)	Completed 2.3.44. In service with US Army. 10.11.44 Portsmouth Command. 15.12.44 reallocated to C in C Nore's Special Pool. 13.1.45 To D of ST at Portsmouth. 7.12.45 arrived Gibraltar and allocated to SNSO as C688. 30.4.53 for disposal. Sold to S Bezzina & Sons Malta, renamed SABE. 1963 Converted to diesel.

TID 57	Completed 29.2.44. In service with US Army. 1.11.44 laid up. 15.12.44 allocated to C in C Nore's Special Pool. January 1945 to D of ST. 29.1.45 sailed for Rosyth—allocated to C D. 16.9.58 sold to MacLellan Ltd for scrap.
TID 59	Completed 7.2.44. In service with 21 Army Group 10.11.44 at Boulogne. 5.2.45 C in C Nore's Pool at Calais. 29.6.45 to D of ST. 6.10.45 naval service at Portland. 13.12.45 naval service at Falmouth. 7.9.46 to Messrs Tamlyn & Co Ltd, Plymouth for C & M. 1947 sold to J Carney, Sunderland. Renamed SUNNYSIDE and converted to diesel. 1965 sold to Brittania Steam Towing, Swansea. Renamed TROVER. Resold to private individual at Menai Straits and renamed LADY OF MENAI.
TID 61	Completed 7.3.44. In service with US Army. 17.1.45 to D of ST. 21.4.45 allocated to C D Chatham as basin tug. 9.4.58 sold to H G Pounds, Portsmouth. 1961 sold to J D Irving, St Johns, Canada and renamed IRVING ELM. Converted to diesel.
TID 62	Completed 4.5.44. MOWT naval service. 16.3.45 to Portsmouth Pool. 20.9.46 sank under tow by HMS TENACITY off Beachy Head whilst on passage to Sheerness.
TID 68	Completed 17.3.44. In service with US Army. 15.5.45 to D of ST. 8.6.45 to FOIC Southampton. RN manned. July 1945 at Falmouth for salvage duties. 27.2.46 transferred to SASO. Bull Point, Plymouth. 1.4.58 to PAS Devonport—for disposal. 2.6.58 transferred to Portland. 10.7.67 towed by SAMSONIA to Pembroke Dock. 15.12.67 sold to Milford Haven Marine Services. 1968 sold to H G Pounds, Portsmouth and scrapped.
TID 69	Completed 21.3.44. MOWT naval service. 22.2.45 to D of ST. Southampton. 26.3.47 sold to Luke Thomas & Co Ltd. Aden.
TID 70	Completed 31.3.44. In service with US Army. 23.12.44 sank under tow of US tug LT533.
TID 71	Completed 31.3.44. In service with US Army. 10.11.44 to D of ST. 29.12.44 to FOIC London for Royal Victoria Yard, Deptford. 5.1.45 with SVSO towing lighters. 26.6.61 at Chatham—sold to H G Pounds, Portsmouth. 1964 sold to Husbands Shipyard,

	Southampton. Converted to diesel. Renamed ASSURANCE and still in service. (1984).
TID 72	Completed 7.4.44. In service with US Army. 23.12.44 to MOWT. 30.6.45 laid up. 2.10.45 transferred to War Department. 1947 sold to River Wear Commissioners. Renamed EVELYN. 1948 renamed PALLION. 1972 converted to diesel. 1985 still in service on Wear.
TID 73 (DASH- OUND)	Completed 18.4.44. In service with US Army. 28.12.44 laid up. 24.5.45 sold to Dashwood & Partners Ltd. 1949 renamed DASHOUND. 1954 converted to diesel. 30.3.55 purchased by Admiralty and to SORF, Hythe, with civilian crew. 5.2.69 to Portsmouth PAS until relieved by FELICITY in 1970. 15.5.70 sold to H G Pounds, Portsmouth.
TID 75	Completed 24.4.44. MOWT naval service. 10.11.44 in Portsmouth Pool. 17.4.46 sailed to Portland allocated to Captain in Charge. 10.10.60 sold to H G Pounds, Portsmouth. 1965 resold to Husbands Shipyard, Southampton. Converted to diesel. Renamed ADHERENCE and still in service (1984).
TID 76	Completed 1.5.44. In service with US Army. 19.12.44 in naval service managed by Channel Dartmouth Coaling Co. 17.1.48 transferred to Admiralty and shipped to Malta. September 1959 de-equipped at Gibraltar. 18.10.60 sold to H G Pounds, Portsmouth for scrap.
TID 77	Completed 6.5.44. MOWT naval service. 10.11.44 Portsmouth Pool.
TID 80	Completed 19.5.44. MOWT naval service. 16.3.44 Portsmouth Pool. In service at Poole. 3.10.45 transferred to Captain in Charge, Portland. June 1962 sold at Portland to Anglo Diesel Co, London. 1965 scrapped.
TID 81	Completed 26.5.44. MOWT naval service. 10.11.44 Portsmouth Pool operating in Southampton and Shoreham area. April 1946 to Captain in Charge, Portland, thence to Messrs Townsend Bros Ltd for C and M. 11.12.50 sold to Messrs C J King & Sons renamed SEA PRINCE. 1957 sunk in collision.
TID 83	Completed 5.6.44. In service with US Army. 10.11.44 to D of ST. 1945 to Captain of Dockyard, Chatham. 1958 relieved by DIVER. 10.3.61 sold to Mr Williams. Orpington, Kent. Renamed MICHAEL HAMILTON. Converted to diesel and sold incomplete (1966) to

Electro Marine Ltd. London. 1967 scrapped at Erith.

TID 90 — Completed 24.7.44. MOWT naval service. 10.11.44 allocated for service at Ostend. 28.2.46 arrived Plymouth for RNAD Bull Point. July 1947 in C & M at RNAD Bull Point. 11.8.47 sailed for Milford Haven and transferred to RNAD. Also used by SORF Milford Haven. 1952 sold to Lloyds Albert Yard. Operated by Risdon Beazley Ltd and renamed ASHFORD 90. 1953 sold to United Towing Co and renamed YEOMAN. 23.4.63 Scrapped by Hendrik Ido, Ambacht, Holland.

TID 92 — Completed 18.8.44. MOWT naval service. 26.11.44 allocated for service at Rouen. 24.1.45 sailed for Southampton. Allocated to Portsmouth Pool for towing outside port limits. 27.9.48 sold to United Africa Co Ltd for the groundnuts scheme. Renamed TESHI.

TID 97 — Completed 12.9.44. Naval service at Rouen, Ostend and Dover. 16.3.45 allocated to C in C Nore's Pool at Sheerness. November 1945 to C D Chatham. 29.12.62 capsized and sank whilst berthing RFA HEBE at Chatham. 4.1.63 salvaged. 31.10.63 sold to Mr P F Horlock, Mistley, Essex.

TID 98 — Completed 22.9.44. Allocated to C in C Nore's Pool. 9.6.45 to D of ST and prepared for service in the Far East. August 1947 transferred to Government of Burma on arrival at Rangoon. November 1947 sold to Inland Water Transport Board. Rangoon.

TID 99 — Completed 22.9.44. Allocated for service at Rouen. 16.3.45 reallocated to Portsmouth Pool for towage outside port limits. 3.9.57 to C D Portsmouth Dockyard. 11.6.73 sold to H G Pounds, Portsmouth and scrapped.

TID 100 — Completed 22.9.44. In service with 21 Army Group. Coastal Towing. 21.2.49 released from service and boiler cleaned at Sheerness. 7.1.58 sold to Richard Abel & Sons Ltd. Liverpool. Renamed RICHARD ABEL. 1966 scrapped by T W Ward, Barrow.

TID 101 — Completed 22.9.44. Allocated to Portsmouth Pool for towage outside port limits. 12.9.47 reallocated to Malta and shipped in SS PACIFIC RANGER. 1.5.48 in service with BDO Malta. 1.12.53 to CD's Boat Pool. 17.5.62 for auction at Malta. 10.4.64 sold to E Cassar,

Floriana, Malta. Renamed SAN MARCO. 1968 sold to Italian buyer.

TID 102   Completed 2.10.44. MOWT naval service. 12.2.45 to War Department. 20.12.48 sold to Edmund Nuttall. Renamed NUTTALL. 1953 sold to Elder Dempster Lines Ltd and allocated to their subsidiary company West Africa Lighterage and Transport Co Ltd. Retained the name NUTTALL.

TID 106   Completed 1.11.44. MOWT naval service. 10.11.44 to Portsmouth Pool. 16.10.45 transferred to RNAD Priddys Hard. Civilian crew. 1.4.53 sold to Messrs Dashwood & Partners Ltd and renamed TIDTUG. 1954 acquired by Elder Dempster Lines Ltd and renamed NUPE. 1955 sold to the Government of Sierra Leone, Freetown.

TID 107   Completed 10.11.44. Allocated to C in C Nore's Pool, Harwich. Coastal towing and with SORF Harwich. 30.12.57 transferred to C D Chatham. 5.1.68 sold to T W Ward Ltd. 1973 sold to Mr B Pearce of Malden. 1976 scrapped at Sittingborne.

TID 109   Completed 8.1.45. Allocated to C in C Nore's Special Pool. 9.6.45 to D of ST for tropicalization. August 1947 arrived Rangoon and transferred to Government of Burma. November 1947 sold to Inland Water Transport Board, Rangoon.

TID 112   Completed 1.3.45. MOWT naval service. 4.6.45 shipped to Calcutta. 25.5.46 sold to Calcutta Port Commissioners.

TID 119   Completed 2.1.45. Allocated to C in C Nore's Special Pool. 16.2.45 arrived Flushing. British crew relieved by Dutch crew. 28.9.46 arrived Portsmouth—towed by HMS TENACITY. Allocated to Civil Engineer's Department. 13.2.46 sold to Messrs Van Den Bosche & Co Antwerp.

TID 122   Completed 26.1.45. Arrived Singapore 18.6.45. 4.10.45 allocated to C D Hong Kong, shipped in EMPIRE CHARNIAN. 15.6.48 transferred to SVSO Hong Kong. 11.9.58 sold to Yau Wing & Co Ltd Hong Kong renamed YAU TUEN.

TID 123   Completed 5.2.45. Shipped to Far East. 4.8.45 at
(C742)   Manus. Allocated to Hong Kong and shipped in EMPIRE CHARNIAN. To DAS Hong Kong. 31.1.47 transferred to SNSO Hong Kong. 11.4.49 renumbered

C742. 28.12.59 sold to Tai Chiong, Kowloon.

TID 124   Completed 6.2.45. Shipped to Far East. 4.8.45 at Manus. Allocated to Hong Kong and shipped in EMPIRE CHARNIAN. To C D Hong Kong. 28.12.59 sold to Tai Chiong, Kowloon.

TID 127   Completed 31.5.45. Shipped in EMPIRE MARSHAL to Hong Kong. Under MOWT on harbour duties for Hong Kong Harbour Board. 4.9.48 sold to Hong Kong and Whampoa Dock Co. ____

TID 128   Completed 8.6.45. Shipped in EMPIRE MARSHAL from Liverpool to Hong Kong. Under MOWT on harbour duties for Hong Kong Harbour Board. 4.9.48 sold to Asiatic Petroleum Co Ltd Hong Kong.

TID 129   Completed 17.2.45. August 1945 at Manus, shipped in EMPIRE CHARNIAN to Hong Kong. To C D Hong Kong. 11.9.58 sold to Wah Hing Metal Co, Kowloon.

TID 130   Completed 24.3.45. Shipped to Far East. August 1945 at Manus. Shipped in EMPIRE CHARNIAN to Hong Kong and to C D Hong Kong. 28.12.59 sold to Tai Chiong & Co.

TID 133   Completed 30.3.45. Allocated to Calcutta. 1946 sold by Indian Disposals Board.

TID 135   Completed 9.4.45. Shipped from Liverpool to Rangoon for Government of Burma. November 1947 sold to Inland Water Transport Board, Rangoon.

TID 136 (BAND-UKI)   Completed 12.4.45. Shipped to Colombo for Rangoon. 5.4.46 at Colombo. March 1947 at Rangoon with Government of Burma. Lifted in SS BELRAY to Kilindini (Mombasa) for RNAD. 20.3.48 renamed locally BANDUKI. 28.4.60 sold to East Africa Marketing Co Ltd Nairobi.

TID 137   Completed 28.4.45. Shipped from Liverpool to Colombo for Rangoon. 5.4.46 at Colombo. 15.4.46 at Rangoon with Government of Burma. February 1948 sold to Tanganyika Railways. 1951 sold to East Africa Railways and Harbours Board. Renamed TOROKA.

TID 138   Completed 28.4.45. June 1945 shipped to Rangoon for Government of Burma. February 1948 sold to Tanganyika Railways. 1951 sold to East African Railways and Harbours Board. Renamed TAVETA.

TID 139   Completed 28.4.45. June 1945 shipped to Rangoon for Government of Burma. November 1947 sold to Inland Water Transport Board, Rangoon.

TID 140   Completed 14.5.45. Shipped from Liverpool and arrived Rangoon 22.9.45. 28.1.48 lifted in SS BELRAY to Trincomalee for reserve. November 1948 sold to East African Railways and Harbours Board. Renamed TIDDLER.

TID 142   Completed 14.5.45. Allocated to C in C Nore's Special Pool. June 1945 shipped from Liverpool. 7.12.45 in service at Gibraltar. 8.2.46 at Singapore for dockyard service. 12.11.69 sold to Siong Huat Hardware Co Ltd. Singapore. 1970 sold to Straits Engineers—converted to diesel, renamed JARAM.

TID 144   Completed 29.5.45. Shipped in EMPIRE MARSHAL. 8.2.46 at Singapore under SASO. 16.6.71 transferred to Singapore Government. 7.4.72 sold to Straits Engineers, Singapore and converted to diesel. Renamed MUTIARA II.

TID 145   Completed 31.5.45. Shipped in EMPIRE MARSHAL. 8.2.46 at Singapore under SASO. 28.8.71 transferred to Singapore Government. 7.4.72 sold to Straits Engineers, Singapore and converted to diesel. Renamed STRAITS ENDURANCE.

TID 146   Completed 14.6.45. Shipped in EMPIRE MARSHAL. 8.2.46 on commercial duties (under MOWT) for Hong Kong Harbour Board. 4.9.48 sold to Taikoo Dockyard & Engineering Co Ltd. Renamed TAIKOO FU. 1968 sold for scrap.

TID 147   Completed 28.6.45. 16.7.45 sailed Hull to Liverpool and shipped in EMPIRE MARSHAL for MOWT Singapore. 24.4.48 sold to John Manners & Co, Hong Kong. 29.7.49 wrecked—total loss.

TID 148   Completed 3.7.45. Shipped in EMPIRE MARSHAL. 8.2.46 to Hong Kong Harbour Board on commercial duties with Wharf Company (under MOWT). 4.9.48 sold to Asiatic Petroleum Co Ltd. Hong Kong. Renamed TSING SHAN. Later sold to Lu Bros (Hong Kong) Ltd. September 1959 sold to Shell Co, Hong Kong

TID 149   Completed 12.7.45. Shipped in EMPIRE MARSHAL to Singapore. 31.5.46 at Inner Roads, Singapore under SVSO. 5.4.47 Under C D Singapore. 3.4.71 transferred to Singapore Government. 7.4.72 sold to Straits Engineers Singapore. Converted to diesel and renamed STRAITS PROGRESS.

TID 150   Completed 16.7.45 for MOWT. 1947 sold to Harris Barges, Liverpool and renamed CRAGDALE. 1949 acquired by Elder Dempster Lines Ltd and renamed NESTON. Shipped in heavy lift ship MARY KINGSLEY to Lagos, Nigeria.

TID 151   Completed 25.7.45. 18.8.45 sailed from Hull to Liverpool and shipped to Singapore in EMPIRE MARSHAL. Transferred to Colonial Government of Hong Kong. December 1947 sold to Hong Kong and Kowloon Wharf Ltd. Renamed PENGUINE.

TID 164   Completed 28.11.45. Naval service at Port Edgar attached to HMS LOCHINVAR. General harbour duties. 12.12.62 in reserve at Rosyth. 5.5.67 brought forward under C D Rosyth. 10.6.74 sold to Medway Maritime Museum, Kent. 1985 lying at Faversham.

TID 165   Completed 18.12.45. Naval service. 1950 at Rosyth attached to HMS SAFEGUARD towing mooring lighters etc. 1961 in reserve—replaced by DIVER. 28.3.62 brought forward to supply steam to C609. 5.12.69 sold to Thomas Ward and scrapped at Inverkeithing.

TID 172   Completed 13.2.46. Nore Command under NOIC
(MAR-   Lowestoft with the name MARTELLO. 11.7.46 reverted
TELLO)   to TID 172 with civilian crew. 20.10.46 allocated to
(W92)   Civil Engineer in Chief, Chatham as W92. 1.10.59 transferred to PAS Chatham as TID 172. 1967 used as relief small tug. 9.7.73 sold to T W Ward Ltd, Grays. 4.8.73 sold to Mr B Pearce of Maldon for preservation.

TID 164

TANACS
All built in Canada during 1944 to similar design with minor variations.The word TANAC was probably derived from T = Tug ANAC = part of the word CANADA in reverse.

Length 65' **Beam** 17' **Draught** 6' **Fuel** 12 tons **GRT** 67 tons **Speed** about 9 knots **Engines** Diesel **HP** 220-270 depending on engine fitted. **Propulsion** Single screw **Complement** 5.

Notes

TANAC 13   February 1944 at Augusta, Sicily. September 1945 at Malta under Director of Stores, 11.12.50 sold to Messrs Mamo Bros (1939) Ltd, Msida, Malta.

TANAC 21   March 1959 at Malta and transferred to Baileys, Malta. Renamed COMINO.

TANAC 25   21.11.46 at Trincomalee, Ceylon. 22.6.53 on loan to NASO Trincomalee. April 1958 shipped to RAF Gan in BEN WYVIS and transferred to Air Ministry.

TANAC 35   Built by German and Milne, Montreal, Canada. Engine, Crossley HRN 3 HP 270. 10.1.48 transferred from British Army custody (Venice) to the Royal Navy at Malta and allocated to the Captain of Dockyard for general harbour duties. 7.4.66 arrived Portsmouth (towed by TYPHOON) to replace TID 32 on general towing duties at Portsmouth. October 1973 for sale at Pembroke Dock. 1.11.73 sold to H G Pounds, Portsmouth.

TANAC 36   Engine, Vivian Diesel ME 270 HP. 10.1.48 transferred from British Army custody (Venice) to Royal Navy at Malta—in reserve. March 1948 transferred to War Office for Marchwood.

TANAC 37   Built 1944. Engine, Diesel Vivian ME 270 HP. January 1948 transferred from British Army custody (Venice) to RN at Malta. Service with BDO later to C D Malta. August 1962 towed by SAMSONIA to Gibraltar to replace TID 56. 3.12.69 sold to W J Harris.

TANAC 56   Engine Crossley HRN 3 270 HP. 28.12.45 at Malta under CD. 6.8.68 sold to Mediterranean Salvage and Towage Co Ltd, Malta. Renamed IRISH TERRIER.

TANAC 58   Engine Crossley HRN 3 270 HP. January 1946 transferred from Venice to Victualling Department Malta. 1953 transferred to C D Malta. 27.11.68 sold to Mediterranean Salvage and Towage Co Ltd, Malta. Renamed SCOTTISH TERRIER.

TANAC 59   Engine Crossley HRN 3 270 HP. January 1946 transferred from Venice to DAS Malta. 1.12.53 transferred to BDO. 18.3.60 transferred to PAS 27.11.68 sold to Mid Med Towage Co Ltd, Malta. Renamed ST THOMAS.

TANAC's at Malta (1961) alongside Sabi

TANAC 60   Engine Crossley HRN 3. 270 HP. January 1946
             transferred from Venice to RNAD, Malta. 1.12.53
             transferred to CD. 6.8.68 sold to Mid Med Towage
             Co Ltd, Malta. Renamed ST MICHAEL.

TANAC 80   January 1946 transferred from Venice to CD
             Malta. 12.4.47 sunk. Subsequently raised and
             repaired. 23.3.59 transferred to Baileys, Malta.
             Renamed FILFLA.

TANAC 83   Built by Central Bridge Co, Trenton, Ontario,
             Canada. Transferred to C D Malta January 1946
             from Venice. Towed to Gibraltar September 1962
             to replace TID II. Sold at Pembroke 10.8.79.

TANAC 90   At Aden January 1946. Embarked in HMS
             EASTWAY 1946 for Singapore.

TANAC 94   Built by Industrial Shipbuilding Co. Canada.
             13.8.45 arrived Aden 31.3.46 shipped to Singapore
             in HMS EASTWAY 31.3.46. November 1947 sold at
             Singapore to Anglo Saxon Petroleum Co.

TANAC 95   Built by Industrial Shipbuilding Co, Canada.
             Vivian Diesel ME 240 HP. Shipped in SS HART
             CRANE to Durban for passage under own power
             to Kilindini (Mombasa). At Durban 6.6.45 and sold
             9.5.47 (presumably) at Durban.

TANAC 99   Built by Smith and Rhuland, Vivian Diesel ME240
             HP. At Calcutta 1.9.45. Declared surplus and for
             disposal 3.5.46.

TANAC 100 Built by Smith and Rhuland. Arrived Aden 13.8.45.
March 1946 shipped in HMS EASTWAY for
Victualling Department Singapore. 8.12.47 sold to
Hiva Giap & Co Singapore.

TANAC 105 Built by Canadian Bridge Co Ltd, Vivian Diesel
ME 240 HP. At Trincomalee, Ceylon under Captain
Superintendant. 8.4.47. January 1958 sold to
Ceylon Government.

TANAC 112 Built by Canadian Bridge Co Ltd. At Cochin 1945.
Selected to bear the name HMS LANDLOCK as
nominal depot ship. 10.4.47 declared surplus and
sold to Baroda State.

TANAC 116 Built by Canadian Bridge Co Ltd. Allocated to C
in CBPF and shipped to Sydney in SS LOUIS
HENNEPIN from New York on 7.3.45. Arrived
Sydney 27.4.45. 7.5.47 sold by Commonwealth
Disposal Mission.

TANAC 117 Allocated to C in CBPF Sydney: Shipped in
JAMES B.ASWELL to Melbourne. Arrived 2.6.45.
January 1948 sold by Commonwealth Disposal
Mission to Geelong Harbour Trust.

TANAC 118 Built by Canadian Bridge Co Ltd. Allocated to C
in C East Indies. Shipped in SS HART CRANE to
Durban for Kilindini. 6.6.45 at Durban awaiting lift
to Calcutta for disposal. Sold 9.5.47.

TANAC 119 Built by Canadian Bridge Co Ltd. 5.4.45 shipped in SS KAIPAKI from New York to Sydney for C in CBPF. 20.11.45 allocated to Hong Kong and sailed under own power.

TANAC 120 Built by Canadian Bridge Co Ltd. Allocated to C in CBPF and shipped from New York on 5.4.45 in SS KAIPAKI to Sydney. 20.11.45 allocated Hong Kong and sailed under own power. 12.4.46 on commercial duties with Wharf Company under MWT. 4.9.48 sold to Hong Kong & Kowloon Wharf & Godown Co Ltd.

TANAC 121 Built by Canadian Bridge Co Ltd. 270 HP engine. Allocated C in CBPF Sydney. 7.3.45 shipped in LOUIS HENNEPIN from New York. Re-allocated to Hong Kong and shipped in EMPIRE CHARNIAN 4.10.45. At RNAD Hong Kong for towage of lighters. 25.5.72 sold to Mr Pang, Hong Kong.

TANAC 125 Built by Canadian Bridge Co Ltd. Engine—Atlas Imperial 6HM 1125, 250 HP. At Calcutta 1.9.45. Sold.

TANAC 127 Built by Canadian Bridge Co Ltd. Shipped in RED GAUNTLET to Calcutta for C in CEI. December 1945 at Singapore. July 1947 sold to KHIM HOE & Co Singapore.

TANAC 128 Built by Canadian Bridge Co Ltd. Shipped in RED GAUNTLET to Calcutta for C in CEI. December 1945 at Singapore, (Loyang) with BDO. February 1948 sold at Singapore to John Manners and Co Hong Kong.

TANAC 129 Engine Atlas Imperial 220 HP. Shipped in AUGUSTUS S MERRIMAN to Calcutta for C in CEI. December 1946 at Singapore. February 1948 sold to John Manners & Co Hong Kong.

TANAC 131 Built by Central Bridge Co Ltd. Engine Vivian Diesel ME 240 HP. Allocated to C in CEI. 10.4.45 at Calcutta. 9.6.45 at Rangoon under Port Commissioners Rangoon. Sold.

TANAC 132 As for TANAC 131.

TANAC 133 Built by Central Bridge Co Ltd. Allocated to C in CBPF and shipped in EMPIRE CHARNIAN to Manus 5.6.45. Commissioned at Manus under SBNO. February 1946 transferred to Hong Kong Harbour Board.

TANAC 134	Built by Central Bridge Co Ltd. Engine—Vivian Diesel ME 240 HP. 5.6.45 shipped in EMPIRE CHARNIAN allocated to SBNO Manus. 21.6.45 commissioned at Manus. May 1946 transferred to MOWT. 27.1.49 sold to Queensland Government through Commonwealth Disposal Mission.
TANAC 135	Engine—Vivian Diesel ME 240 HP. December 1944 at Sydney allocated to C in CBPF. May 1946 allocated to Colonial Government. 17.9.49 sold to Hong Kong Colonial Goverment.
TANAC 136	Built by Central Bridge Co Ltd. Engine—Vivian Diesel ME 240 HP. 5.6.45 shipped in EMPIRE CHARNIAN for C in CBPF. 4.7.45 commissioned at Manus. May 1946 transferred to MOWT. August 1948 sold through Commonwealth Disposal Mission.
TANAC 148	Built by Central Bridge Co Ltd. Engine-Vivian Diesel ME 240 HP. 1.9.45 allocated to C in CEI at Cochin. 4.9.48 declared surplus. To Indian Disposal Mission.
TANAC 149	November 1946 at Ceylon. June 1948 sold to China Navigation Co Ltd, Hong Kong.
TANAC 150	Built by Central Bridge Co Ltd 1944. Engine—Vivian Diesel ME 240 HP. Allocated to C in CEI at Cochin. Commissioned as nominal depot ship HMS LANDSWELL. 1.9.45 at Trincomalee allocated to FO Ceylon. 5.6.47 with Director of Stores, Trincomalee. 11.4.49 vessel renumbered C721 and employed on Fleet Fuelling Service. Sold November 1959 (probably to Indian Navy).
TANAC 153	Built by Central Bridge Co Ltd. Engine Vivian Diesel ME 240 HP. Allocated to C in CBPF and shipped from New York, 7.3.45 in SS LOUIS HENNEPIN. 27.4.45 arrived Sydney. 1.7.45 commissioned as HMS WOOLLOOMOOLOO. May 1946 allocated to Colonial Government. 17.9.49 sold to Hong Kong Colonial Government.

TANAC 154
(C720)
Built by Central Bridge Co Ltd. Engine—Vivian Diesel ME 240 HP. June 1945 allocated to C in CEI at Bombay. 1946 at Trincomalee. 5.6.47 with Director of Stores 11.4.49 vessel renumbered C720 for Fleet Fuelling Service. July 1959 sold (probably to Indian Navy).

TANAC 155
Built by Central Bridge Co Ltd. Engine—Vivian Diesel ME 240 HP. 7.3.45 allocated C in CBPF Sydney and shipped in SS LOUIS HENNEPIN from New York. 27.4.45 arrived Sydney. May 1946 transferred to MOWT. January 1948 sold by Commonwealth Disposal Mission to Mr Carpenter & Co Ltd Sydney.

TANAC 156
Engine—Vivian Diesel ME 240 HP. Allocated to C in CBPF Sydney and shipped in SS JAMES B ASWELL. 2.6.45 arrived Sydney. May 1946 transferred to MOWT. August 1948 sold through Commonwealth Disposal Mission.

TANAC 157
Built by Central Bridge Co Ltd. Engine—Vivian Diesel ME 240 HP. 10.4.45 at Calcutta. 1.9.45 at Vizagapatam. December 1945 at Trincomalee with Victualling Supply Officer. 9.10.53 approved for disposal locally.

TANAC 159
Built by Central Bridge Co Ltd. Engine—Vivian Diesel ME 240 HP. Allocated to C in CEI. 10.4.45 at Calcutta. 9.6.45 at Vizagapatam. December 1945 at Trincomalee. 31.3.46 shipped to Singapore in HMS EASTWAY. 28.6.48 sold to Anglo Saxon Petroleum Co Singapore.

TANAC 163
Built by Central Bridge Co Ltd 1944. Engine Vivian Diesel ME 240 HP. 1.9.45 at Trincomalee under D of V and renumbered VSO 14. 4.2.58 sold to Ceylon Navy.

TANAC 172
Built by Central Bridge Co Ltd. Shipped in SS RONDEAU PARK to Sydney (arrived 14.7.45) May 1946 Allocated to Colonial Government. 17.9.49 sold to Hong Kong Government.

TANAC 173
Built by Central Bridge Co Ltd. Shipped in SS RONDEAU PARK to Sydney. (Arrived 14.7.45) May 1946 allocated to Colonial Government. 31.5.46 at Loyang. 11.8.47 at Singapore with CD. 28.6.48 sold to Anglo Saxon Petroleum Co Ltd.

TANAC 175   Allocated to C in CEI and shipped in SS
             AUGUSTUS S MERRIMAN to Calcutta (arrived
             1.8.45) December 1946 at Port Swettenham. 1947
             sold to Eng Hup & Co through the British Stores
             Disposal Mission.
TANAC 184   November 1945 shipped in SS FORT BRANDON
             to Calcutta. Transferred to Burma RNVR at
             Rangoon. 23.1.48 transferred to War Office. 1952
             handed over to Burma Government.
TANAC 185   Built by Canadian Bridge Co Ltd 17.9.45. Shipped
             in SS SAMDAK for C in CEI Bombay. 8.10.45 on
             station. December 1945 at Singapore for dockyard
             service. November 1947 sold to Anglo Saxon
             Petroleum Ltd.
TANAC 186   Built by Canadian Bridge Co Ltd. 17.9.45 shipped
             in SS SAMDAK for C in CEI Bombay. 8.10.45 on
             station. 28.6.49 transferred to Government of
             India.
TANAC 187   Engine Vivian Diesel ME 240 HP. December 1945
             at Singapore under C in CBPF. November 1947
             with the army at Bombay and transferred to the
             War Office.
TANAC 189   Built by Canadian Bridge Co Ltd. Engine Vivian
             Diesel ME 240 HP. December 1945 at Singapore.
             July 1947 sold to Tan Ah Pee.
TANAC 196   Built by Canadian Bridge Co Ltd. Engine Vivian
             Diesel ME. Shipped in SS FORT GRAHAME to
             Karachi (arrived 30.8.45). December 1945 at
             Bombay. 21.3.46 shipped to Singapore. 11.8.47 at
             Singapore under Captain of Dockyard. 11.8.50
             sold locally.
TANAC 197   Built by Canadian Bridge Co Ltd. Engine Vivian
             Diesel ME 240 HP. Shipped in SS FORT
             GRAHAME to Karachi (arrived 30.8.45) 8.9.45 on
             station Bombay. 31.5.46 at Singapore Dockyard.
             28.6.48 sold to Anglo Saxon Petroleum Co Ltd.
TANAC 198   Built by Canadian Bridge Co Ltd. Engine Vivian
             Diesel ME 240 HP. 22.9.45 shipped to Bombay
             and on station. Embarked in HMS EASTWAY for
             Singapore. 8.4.47 at Singapore with Captain of
             Dockyard. 11.8.50 sold locally at Singapore.

Tanac 35 (1968)

TANAC 199   Built by Canadian Bridge Co Ltd. Engine Vivian Diesel ME 240 HP. 22.9.45 shipped to Bombay. 11.8.47 shipped to Singapore in HMS EASTWAY for CD, Singapore. 11.8.50 sold locally.

TANAC 205   Built by Canadian Bridge Co Ltd. Shipped in SS FORT BRANDON to Calcutta (arrived 5.12.45). June 1946 transferred to Burma RNVR at Rangoon. 24.4.48 transferred to War Office and handed over to Government of Burma.

TANAC 214   Shipped New York to Calcutta in SS DE PAUW VICTORY. 1947 transferred to Burma RNVR at Rangoon. 23.1.48 transferred to War Office and handed over to Government of Burma.

TANAC 215   9.11.45 shipped to Calcutta in SS DE PAUW VICTORY. 23.1.48 transferred to War Office and handed over to Government of Burma.

ENVOY CLASS

Ship	Pennant Number	Completion Date	Builder
ENCHANTER	W178	1944	Cochrane & Sons, Selby, Yorkshire
ENCORE	W179 (A379)	1944	" "
ENFORCER	W177	1944	" "
ENIGMA	W175	1944	" "
ENTICER	W166	1944	" "
ENVOY	W165 (A165)	1944	" "

Length 174' 6" **Beam** 36' **Draught** 17' **GRT** 762 **Speed** 13 knots **Engines** steam triple expansion **Fuel** FFO 363 tons **HP** 1625 **Propulsion** Single screw **Bollard Pull** approx 16 tons **Complement** 33.

HM Tug Encore (1945)

HM Tug Enforcer (1950)

HMS Enigma (1944)

Notes

ENCHANTER To commercial use as ENGLISHMAN in 1947. Renamed CINTRA in 1962.

ENCORE 1949 Naval manned. 1958 at Hong Kong civilian manned under RFA conditions. 6.11.67 sold to Selco Ltd, Singapore.

ENFORCER June 1947 under C in C Portsmouth. 1949 civilian manned under RFA conditions. 26.1.50 transferred to Rosyth for sea-going duties. 1963 sold to Jas White & Co Ltd, St Davids Harbour.

ENIGMA 8.4.47 at Singapore as Fleet Target Towing and Rescue Tug. 13.10.52 modified for harbour work. 26.7.62 commissioned and sailed for Plymouth. 8.10.62 arrived Plymouth and paid off. 1965 sold to Greek commercial interests and renamed VERNICOS.

ENTICER Based Hong Kong, Manned by UK Yardcraft Officers and locally entered crew. 12.12.46 lost in heavy weather in the South China Sea going to the assistance of SS ROSEBANK.

ENVOY 1949 civilian manned under RFA conditions. 1965 sold to Loucas Matsas & Sons, Piraeus, Greece. Renamed MATSAS.

SAMSON CLASS

Ship	Pennant Number	Completion Date	Builder	Based
SAMSON	A390	1954	Alex Hall	Portsmouth
SEA GIANT	A288	1955	" "	Malta, Devonport Portland
SUPERMAN	—	1954	" "	Devonport

Length 180′ 6″ **Beam** 36′ 11″ **Draught** 17′ 6″ **GRT** 854 **Speed** 15 knots **Engines** Steam reciprocating. **Boilers** 2 x water tube, Babcock & Wilcox. Oil fired. **Fuel** FFO 316 tons. **HP** 3000 **Propulsion** Twin screws, single rudder. **Bollard Pull** 30 tons **Range** 5000 miles at 12 knots **Complement** 30.

HM Tug Samson

Notes

These vessels were used mainly for harbour work with occasional sea towing and salvage work. Equipped for firefighting, salvage and oil pollution spraying. Fitted with towing winches.

SAMSON 1974 laid up at Portsmouth. Sale to Chilean Navy not finalised. 29.4.77 sold to H G Pounds.

SEA GIANT 1955 allocated to C D Malta. 12.3.65 arrived Devonport to relieve CAREFUL. 11.7.68 reallocated to Portland to relieve ANTIC for target towing duties. 24.6.70 hit by shell from German destroyer "Schleswig-Holstein" during exercises off Portland. 4.7.80 taken out of service at Portland. 8.11.80 towed from Portland to be broken up at Gijon (Spain).

SUPERMAN 6.12.79 sold to Desquaces Heme SA of Gijon (Spain). 12.12.79 towed from Devonport to Spain to be broken up.

RMAS Sea Giant

CONFIANCE CLASS

Ship	Pennant Number	Completion Date	Builder
ACCORD	A90	1958	A & J Inglis
ADVICE	A89	1959	A & J Inglis
AGILE	A88	1959	Goole S B Co
CONFIANCE	A289	1956	A & J Inglis
CONFIDENT	A290	1956	A & J Inglis

Length 140' **Beam** 37' **Draught** 13' 7" **GRT** 650 **Speed** 13 knots **Engines** PAXMAN 12 YHAXM x 4. **BHP** 1600 **Propulsion** Twin controllable pitch propellers, single rudder. **Bollard Pull** 24.6 tons **Range** Over 5000 miles @ 13 knots **Complement** 22.

HM Tug Accord (1956)

HM Tug Advice

Notes

Fitted for firefighting, salvage and with a towing winch. Used for both harbour and sea towing duties but not popular at sea due to their "extreme liveliness" in rough weather.

ACCORD Based Devonport until 24.6.66 then Rosyth. 17.7.68 transferred to Clyde. 1977 returned to Rosyth. 1985 placed in reserve.

ADVICE Based Devonport manned under RFA conditions 1963 to Singapore for PAS. 1.11.71 sailed for Devonport towing SPANIEL. 6.7.83 to Portland vice CONFIANCE. 1984 for disposal at Portland. 1985 sunk as a target.

AGILE Based Portsmouth manned under RFA conditions to relieve PROSPEROUS. 1960 towed REWARD to Malta. 1964 in reserve at Pembroke Dock. October 1964 brought into service and manned under RFA conditions. Sailed for Singapore and arrived 19.10.65 to replace ENCORE. 1967 returned to UK towing FROSTY from Malta to Rosyth. 1971 transferred to Portsmouth vice CAPABLE as a relief tug. June 1981 transferred to Gibraltar vice ROBUST.

CONFIANCE Based Portsmouth until 1957 then Malta until 1960. Returned to Portsmouth until 1966 then re-allocated to Devonport. 25.7.84 sunk as a target in the North Sea.

CONFIDENT Based Devonport until 1957 then Gibraltar to replace RETORT. Re-allocated to Portsmouth from 9.5.74. •

HM Tug Agile (1965)

HM Tug Typhoon

TYPHOON CLASS

Ship	Pennant Number	Completion Date	Builder
TYPHOON	A95	1960	Henry Robb

Length 60m, 196′ 8″ **Beam** 12m, 39′ 4″ **Draught** 4m, 13′ 1″ **GRT** 1034 **Speed** 15 knots **Engines** Vickers Armstrong (ASRI) x 2 **BHP** 2750 **Propulsion** Single controllable pitch propeller **Bollard Pull** 33 tons **Range** 15000 miles @ 12 knots **Complement** 27.

Notes
Designed for ocean towing, rescue, salvage and firefighting.
1982 sailed for the Falklands Island with the RN Task Force.
Manned under RFA conditions until included in the RMAS.
 Now (1985) based on the Clyde—but expected to be retired shortly.

RMAS Collie

DOG CLASS

Ship	Pennant Number	Completion Date	Builder
AIREDALE	A102	1961	R Dunston
ALSATIAN	A106	1961	" "
BEAGLE BASSET from 3.6.65	A327	1963	" "
BOXER FOXHOUND from 21.10.77	A326	1963	" "
CAIRN	A126	1965	J S Doig

RMAS Pointer

Ship	Pennant Number	Completion Date	Builder
COLLIE	A328	1964	Rowhedge Ironworks. Colchester
CORGI	A330	1965	" "
DALMATIAN	A129	1965	J S Doig
DEERHOUND	A155	1966	Appledore Shipbuilding Co
ELKHOUND	A162	1966	" "
HUSKY	A178	1969	" "
LABRADOR	A168	1966	" "
MASTIFF	A180	1967	" "
POINTER	A188	1967	" "
SALUKI	A182	1969	" "
SEALYHAM	A197	1967	" "
SETTER	A189	1969	" "
SHEEPDOG	A250	1969	" "
SPANIEL	A201	1967	" "

Length 94' **Beam** 24' 3" **Draught** 12' **GRT** 151.65 **Speed** 10.5 knots
Engines Lister Blackstone ERS 8 MGR x 2. **BHP** 1320 **Propulsion**
twin screws (twin rudders) **Bollard Pull** 16.1 tons **Range** 2,200 miles
@ 10 knots. **Complement** 7.

Notes
These small, powerful and very manoeuvrable tugs have proved
themselves extremely useful. Fitted for firefighting and with salvage
pumps but not with towing winches. As duty tugs in the Dockyards
they are called upon to cover many emergency and routine tows.
   Masts can be lowered for working under sponsons of aircraft
carriers and any ship with over-hanging superstructure.

AIREDALE	Based at Malta until 1961 then Gibraltar. 1985 transferred to civilian use at Gibraltar Dockyard.
ALSATIAN	Based at Devonport then Portland.
BEAGLE	Based at Portland.
BOXER	Based at Portsmouth. — RE NAMED FOXHOUND
CAIRN	Based at Rosyth (replaced INTEGRITY).
COLLIE	Based at Chatham (replaced ENERGETIC) until 1.8.83 then Rosyth.
CORGI	Based at Rosyth (replaced ENERGY) then Devonport.
DALMATIAN	Based at Postsmouth.
DEERHOUND	Based at Clyde.
ELKHOUND	Based at Clyde. Arrived Rosyth 22.9.66 to replace HANDMAID.
HUSKY	Based at Clyde (Faslane).
LABRADOR	Based at Clyde (Faslane).
MASTIFF	Based at Chatham until 3.10.83 then Devonport.
POINTER	Based at Rosyth.
SALUKI	Based at Devonport.
SEALYHAM	Towed to Gibraltar 9.6.67 by SAMSONIA to replace VAGRANT.
SETTER	Based at Chatham/Portsmouth.
SHEEPDOG	Based at Portland.
SPANIEL	Based at Devonport & Singapore. 1.11.71 towed from Singapore to Gibraltar by ADVICE. Clyde (Faslane) from 3.6.72.

RMAS Foxhound

RMAS Agatha

GIRL CLASS

Ship	Pennant Number	Completion Date	Builder
AGATHA	A116	1961	P K Harris & Sons
AGNES	A121	1961	" "
ALICE	A113	1961	" "
AUDREY	A117	1961	" "
BARBARA	A324	1963	R Dunston
BETTY	A323	1963	" "
BRENDA	A325	1963	" "
BRIDGET	A322	1963	" "

Length 61' 6" **Beam** 17' **Draught** 7' 6" **GRT** 37.88 **Speed** 10 knots **Engines** Lister Blackstone ERS 6MR. **BHP** 495 **Propulsion** Single Screw **Bollard Pull** 6.5 tons **Range** 1000 miles **Complement** 4.

RMAS Bridget

Notes

Rather small for their power and best used in harbour towing lighters and other light towage.

AGATHA	Based Portland until sold to Itchen Marine Towage Ltd, Hants, in November 1982. Renamed WYETOW.
AGNES	Based Portland. 23.7.83 sold to J P Knight Ltd, Rochester.
ALICE	Based Pembroke Dock until sold (Sept 82) to Holyhead Towing Co. Renamed AEON CEFNI.
AUDREY	Based Devonport and Rosyth. (Nov 82) Sold to Coastal Launch Services Ltd, Hants.
BARBARA	Based Rosyth. 1967 towed to Chatham by ACCORD. March 1983 sold to H G Pounds, Portsmouth.
BETTY	Based Chatham. December 1983 transferred to Medway Ports Authority.
BRENDA	Based Devonport & Chatham. 28.7.83 transferred to MOD (Army) at Marchwood.
BRIDGET	Based Portsmouth. August 1983 transferred to MOD (Army) at Marchwood.

IMPROVED GIRL CLASS

Ship	Pennant Number	Completion Date	Builder
CELIA	A206	1966	Isaac Pimblott Northwich
CHARLOTTE	A210	1966	" '
CHRISTINE	A217	1966	" "
CLARE	A218	1967	" "
DAISY	A145	1968	R Dunston
DAPHNE	A156	1968	" "
DORIS	A252	1969	" "
DOROTHY	A173	1969	" "
EDITH	A177	1969	" "

Length 72′ 6″ **Beam** 20′ 6″ **Draught** 8′ 2′ **GRT** 76.61 **Speed** 10 knots **Engines** Lister Blackstone ERS 6 MGR. **BHP** 495 **Propulsion** Single Screw **Bollard Pull** 6 tons **Range** 2000 miles at 10 knots **Complement** 4.

Notes
Using the same engine power as the GIRL class tugs, the larger hull improved performance particularly when towing from the hook.

Used for towing lighters, assisting larger tugs with cold moves and assisting ships berthing.

RMAS Doris

CELIA	7.9.66 shipped in M/V MENELAUS to Singapore. 3.4.71 transferred to Singapore Government.
CHARLOTTE	Based at Devonport then Portsmouth (1983).
CHRISTINE	Based at Devonport.
CLARE	Based at Singapore then Hong Kong (Naval manned) left Birkenhead as deck cargo on M/V NELEUS 6.2.68.
DAISY	Based at Clyde (Faslane).
DAPHNE	Based at Clyde then Portland.
DORIS	Based at Devonport.
DOROTHY	Based at Hong Kong 31.7.69 to 1.4.79 then transferred to Portsmouth.
EDITH	Based at Gibraltar.

RMAS Roysterer

"R" CLASS

Ship	Pennant Number	Completion Date	Builder
ROBUST	A366	1972	C D Holmes
ROLLICKER	A502	1973	" "
ROYSTERER	A361	1971	" "

Length 54m, 177′ **Beam** 12m, 39′ 4″ **Draught** 6m, 19′ 8″ **GRT** 1036 **Speed** 15 knots **Engines** Mirrlees KMR 6 x 2 **BHP** 4,500 **Propulsion** Twin controllable pitch propellers. Twin rudders **Bollard Pull** 50 tons **Range** 12,300 miles @ 12 knots **Complement** 28.

Notes

Designed for ocean towing, firefighting, salvage and harbour duties. The original design was 'shortened' by some 30′ (to save money) giving them a somewhat squat appearance. The twin C P propellers provide quick manoeuvring and allow the application of full power under all towing conditions. The twin rudders give excellent steering and are particularly beneficial if the vessel has to operate with only one screw.

Previous twin screw tugs fitted with only one rudder found great difficulty in maintaining station with other tugs when towing ahead of heavy tows.

Replacements for BUSTLER and SAMSON class tugs.

Lifeboats were removed. Replaced by inflatable rafts during the 'Cod War' when it was feared they would "ice up" and result in too much top weight. Lifeboats were later replaced by liferafts (from all ships carrying them) throughout the RMAS fleet.

ROBUST based Gibraltar until February 1977 then returned to Devonport to replace SUPERMAN. ROYSTERER based Devonport. ROLLICKER based Portland (1985).

The RMAS tugs Robust & Rollicker tow HMS Eagle from Devonport to the breakers Oct 1978.

PADDLE TUGS

Paddle tugs were quite versatile craft but were most useful for:-
1. Securing alongside aircraft carriers—under their overhanging flight decks—to provide power for cold moves or to transfer men and stores.
2. Securing alongside vessels of all kinds (except submarines) to provide power for cold moves (ie the movements of a vessel without its own power).
3. Carrying large numbers of passengers (together with the necessary additional lifesaving equipment). The large deck spaces available and the "browing facilities" made them ideal for this.

When secured alongside another vessel for a cold move the paddle tug would be tightly secured and parallel to the vessel so that the paddle wheels would be abeam of the vessel's natural turning point. In this way the inside paddle could produce forward or reverse movement of the tow and the outboard paddle could be used to influence direction. Ships of destroyer/frigate size could generally be moved with the assistance of only a small tug.

Paddle tugs could also tow from towing hooks but were not quite as efficient in this way as a conventional screw tug.

In harbour paddle wheels were used independently but for safety at sea it was necessary to clutch the two paddle shafts together to prevent racing should one wheel be lifted out of the water. It also helped to stabilize steering.

These vessels were seaworthy but the paddle wheels were prone to damage on long voyages either by striking floating objects or the wooden blades working loose due to their continuous pounding into the water. The paddle blades were made of a water resistant wood such as Canadian elm and measured approx 12' x 4'. They were feathered by means of a set of eccentric radial arms so that all the time they were in the water they were in a vertical attitude for maximum efficiency.

HM Tug Industrious

DROMEDARY CLASS

Ship	Pennant Number	Completion Date	Builder
ADVICE	W24	1900	London & Glasgow
CRACKER	W19	1900	" "
ENERGETIC	W71	1902	Clydebank
INDUSTRIOUS	W32	1902	Barclay Curle Glasgow
RESTLESS (RESTIVE)		1902	Day & Summers
VOLCANO (VOLATILE)	W61	1900	Barclay Curle, Glasgow

Length 152' **Beam** 54' **Draught** 11' **Displacement** 772 tons loaded **Speed** 10 knots **Engines** Steam reciprocating. Coal fired 103 tons. **HP** 1250 **Propulsion** 2 independent paddle wheels—feathering blades. **Bollard Pull** 9.5 tons **Complement** 18.

Notes

The engines of these tugs were unusual in that each paddle shaft had one crank into which were connected two pistons direct from cylinders mounted in the engine room below so that a triangle was formed with the crank at the apex. As the crank moved around, the huge cylinders oscillated.

INDUSTRIOUS, and possibly some of the others, never had a generator fitted and all lighting was by oil lamp. A sight and sound to be remembered by those who knew them was that of warming through engines on a dark morning. The engine room was lit by strategically placed duck lamps with long flickering smoky flames, four huge cylinders gently rocking in the gloom, two steam reversing engines clattering around with water drains open—hissing steam. Boiler pressure was only 70 lbs per sq in.

The engineers needed considerable skill and anticipation in driving these engines to comply with the Bridge telegraph.

HM Tug Cracker

HM Tug Restive

ADVICE   Based Sheerness under CD. 20.10.50 sold to James Scott & Co (Cork) Ltd.

CRACKER   Based Malta 1911 then Sheerness. July 1956 Scrapped Grays.

ENERGETIC   Based Gibraltar under CD. 13.4.53 sold to British Iron and Steel Corporation (Salvage) Ltd, London for breaking up.

INDUSTRIOUS   Based Devonport under CD. 25.11.59 sold to H G Pounds, Portsmouth. Towed from Portsmouth 5.12.59 for Ymuiden to be broken up.

RESTLESS   Based Malta. 1916 renamed RESTIVE. 1938 for disposal.

VOLCANO   Based Portsmouth under CD. 1914 renamed VOLATILE. 21.3.57 sold for breaking up.

Other vessels of this class were:-

DILIGENT   Completed 1898. Builder Barclay Curle. Disposed of 1924.

DROMEDARY   Completed 1894. Builder Barclay Curle. Disposed of 1925.

ESCORT   Completed 1896. Builder Fawsett. Disposed of 1923.

ROBUST CLASS

Ship	Pennant Number	Completion Date	Builder
CAMEL	W38	1915	Bow McLachlan
FIRM	W15	1911	Chatham Dockyard
GRAPPLER	W26	1908	" "
HELLESPONT	W86	1910	Earle's Ship-building Co
RAMBLER	W80	1909	Clydebank
ROBUST	W28	1907	Bow McLachlan
SPRITE	W53	1915	" "
STRENUOUS (SANDBOY)	W48	1912	Thorneycroft
STURDY (SWARTHY)	W12	1913	" "
VETERAN (ANCIENT)	W54	1915	Thorneycroft

Length 152′ 6″ **Beam** 50′ 6″ **Draught** 11′ **GRT** 412 **Displacement** 635 tons light, 780 tons deep. **Speed** 12 knots **Engines** steam reciprocating double expansion. Coal capacity 103 tons. **IHP** 1250 **Propulsion** 2 independent paddle wheels—feathering blades **Bollard Pull** 10 tons **Compiement** 17.

Notes
An attractive feature of this class (which also applied to PERT) was that their main engines and their driving positions were at main deck level and visible from the deck through square "windows". Four large cranks, pistons and crossheads, always kept in a shining condition, and all moving together in a nearly horizontal plane, were a great attraction to the many passengers carried. It seemed as if such massive and well kept machinery could, and should, have lasted forever.

HM Tug Sprite (1948)

CAMEL   Based Devonport under CD. 15.6.53
Coronation Review Portsmouth. 1962 sold
to Haulbowline Industries Ltd. Co. Cork.

FIRM   Based Sheerness under CD. 7.9.54
transferred to CD Rosyth. 19.8.60 sold to
Messrs Van Den Bosche, Antwerp. Arrived
Antwerp 2.9.60.

GRAPPLER   Based Portsmouth under CD. 1957 sold to
Dover Industries Ltd. Arrived Dover 20.5.57
to be broken up.

HELLESPONT   Based Haulbowline Dockyard, Queenstown,
Ireland until 1922 then Malta. April 1942 lost
at Malta, bombed by Italian aircraft.

RAMBLER   Based Gibraltar under CD. 10.10.49 arrived
Rosyth under tow for service with CD.
13.4.53 sold to British Iron & Steel
Corporation for scrap.

ROBUST   Based Sheerness under CD until 1943 then
Malta. 1957 replaced by DIRECTOR and
scrapped.

HM Tug Swarthy (1947)

SPRITE   Based Portsmouth under CD. 14.3.60 sold
                to H G Pounds, Portsmouth. 27.3.60 arrived
                New Waterway having been resold to Dutch
                breakers.

STRENUOUS   Based Bermuda under CD. 1918 renamed
                SANDBOY. 27.6.47 sunk as a gunnery
                target.

STURDY   Based Portsmouth under CD. 1916 renamed
                SWARTHY. 17.2.61 sold to Haulbowline
                Industries Ltd, Ireland. 24.3.61 arrived
                Passage West, Co Cork.

VETERAN   Based at Malta under CD. 1918 renamed
                ANCIENT. 13.4.53 sold to British Iron and
                Steel Corp for scrap.

PERT CLASS

Ship	Pennant Number	Comp. Date	Builder	Based
PERT	W42	1916	Thorneycroft & Son	Devonport

Length 179′ 6″ **Beam** 59′ **Draught** 12′ **Displacement** 1023 tons **Speed** 13 knots **Engines** Steam double expansion reciprocating. 3 Boilers **IHP** 2000 **Propulsion** 2 independent paddle wheels, feathering blades. **Bollard Pull** approx 20 tons **Complement** 20.

Notes
This unique tug was the largest paddle tug in the Admiralty service and had a very long, and useful, life. Note the band around the funnel which was coloured to indicate the department to which it belonged.
Blue band indicated Captain of Dockyards Dept.
Red band indicated Royal Naval Armament Depot.
Green band indicated Victualling Dept.
White band or white disc with black centre, Naval Stores Dept.
Funnel markings no longer apply. PERT. attended various Reviews at Spithead being ideal for carrying large numbers of passengers. Picture shows her leaving Plymouth for Portsmouth to attend the Coronation Review in June 1953 leading CAMEL, ATLAS, CAREFUL and RECOVERY. October 1961 withdrawn from service. 15.6.62 sold for scrap.

HM Tug Pert leads Camel, Atlas & Careful from Devonport en route to the 1953 Spithead Review.

RMAS Griper

DIRECTOR CLASS

Ship	Pennant Number	Completion Date	Builder
DEXTEROUS	A93	1957	Yarrows, Glasgow
DIRECTOR	A94	1956	" "
FAITHFUL	A85	1957	" "
FAVOURITE	A87	1958	Ferguson, Glasgow
FORCEFUL	A86	1957	Yarrows, Glasgow
GRINDER	A92	1958	Wm Simons, Renfrew
GRIPER	A91	1958	" "

Length 155 ' **Beam** 60' **Draught** 12'**GRT** 472 **Speed** 13 knots
Engines Paxman Diesel 12 YHAXZ x 4 **BHP** 1600 **Propulsion** 2
Electrically driven independent paddle wheels **Bollard Pull** 16
tons **Range** 5,900 miles @ 13 knots. **Complement** 22.

Notes
Fitted for firefighting, salvage and oil pollution spraying. Not
fitted with towing winches.

The electric drive provided a very quick response to the direct
bridge controls and made these tugs a joy to handle.

The masts could be lowered, by hand turning gear, to rest
between the funnels when working under the overhang of aircraft
carriers.

DEXTEROUS   27.2.57 manned by PAS crew and sailed to
Portsmouth. August 1958 sailed to
Devonport and from Devonport, in company
with FAITHFUL, to Gibraltar to relieve
ASSIDUOUS. 24.11.81 sold to Desquaces
del Guadalquiver, Seville, Spain.

DIRECTOR	23.11.56 manned by PAS crew and sailed to Portsmouth. 1957 sailed to Malta and served under CD. Malta with UK PAS Officers and local crew. 10.7.68 arrived Devonport having been towed from Malta by CYCLONE. 22.10.69 sailed to Pembroke Dock and placed in reserve. 13.5.70 arrived Rosyth towed by AGILE to relieve RESOLVE. 18.12.79 sold and towed from Rosyth. 15.5.80 broken up at Gijon (Spain).
FAITHFUL	1957 manned by PAS crew and sailed to Devonport. 1958 sailed from Devonport in company with DEXTEROUS to Gibraltar and thence to Malta for service under CD. 7.9.58 arrived Malta to replace DILIGENT. September 1961 sailed to Devonport for further service under CD Devonport. 4.9.81 withdrawn from service. 12.4.83 sailed from Devonport (towed by ROBUST) to be sunk as a target off Gibraltar. 21.4.83 sunk by HM Ships ALACRITY, BATTLEAXE & BRAZEN.
FAVOURITE	26.9.58 from builder to Devonport under CD. 6.12.79 sold and towed from Devonport 8.1.80. 11.1.80 arrived Gijon (Spain) under tow to be broken up.
FORCEFUL	1957 from builder to Portsmouth under CD. 10.11.81 transferred to DNAW as a missile target at Aberporth Range.
GRINDER	1958 from builder to Portsmouth under CD. 23.9.63 completed Portsmouth refit. New engines fitted. 6.12.79 sold to H G Pounds Portsmouth. 3.3.80 towed from Portsmouth to be broken up at Gijon (Spain).
GRIPER	1958 from builder to Rosyth under CD. 27.1.66 re-allocated to Portsmouth. 6.12.79 sold to H G Pounds Portsmouth. 29.2.80 towed from Portsmouth to be broken up at Gijon (Spain).

RMAS Faithful

TRACTOR TUGS

The introduction of tractor tugs into naval service meant that tug masters had to adapt from handling conventional screw and paddle tugs to the very different handling characteristics of the tractor tugs with their propellers placed in the forward part of the tug. This situation demanded a new line of thought—much like driving on the right hand side of the road after being used to the left. The ability to direct propeller thrust through 360° opened up new ways of undertaking a tow—and gave greater safety.

One principle, however, remained the same and that was when securing alongside a vessel for a cold move the propeller must be kept clear of the vessel being towed so as not to inhibit the flow of water from it.

A very useful asset in these tugs is the capability of being able to steer easily whilst proceeding stern first.

TRITON CLASS

Ship	Penn No.	Comp. Date	Builder	Based
IRENE	A181	1972	R Dunston	Portsmouth
ISABEL	A183	1972	" "	" "
JOAN	A190	1972	" "	" "
JOYCE	A193	1972	" "	Chatham/ Portsmouth
KATHLEEN	A166	1972	" "	Chatham then Pembroke Dock
KITTY	A170	1972	" "	Portsmouth
LESLEY	A172	1973	" "	Chatham until 9.8.83 then Devonport.

RMAS Myrtle

Ship	Penn No.	Comp. Date	Builder	Based
LILAH	A174	1973	R Dunston	Devonport
MARY	A175	1973	" "	" "
MYRTLE	A199	1973	" "	" "
NANCY	A202	1973	" "	" "
NORAH	A205	1973	" "	Portsmouth

Length 60' **Beam** 17' 3" **Draught** 8' 6" **GRT** 50 **Speed** 8 knots **Engines** Lister Blackstone ERS 4 MGR **BHP** 330 **Propulsion** Single Voith Schneider Unit **Bollard Pull** 3.3 tons **Range** 3672 miles @ 8 knots **Complement** 4.

Notes
Used for towing lighters, assisting larger tugs with cold moves and small ships berthing and unberthing under their own power.

FELICITY CLASS

Ship	Penn No.	Comp. Date	Builder	Based
FELICITY	A112	1969	R Dunston	Portsmouth until 1970 Chatham until 27.6.83 then Devonport
FIONA	A148	1973	Hancocks S B Co, Pembroke Dock	Portsmouth
FLORENCE	A149	1980	R Dunston	Devonport
FRANCES	A147	1980	" "	" "
GENEVIEVE	A150	1980	" "	Rosyth
GEORGINA	A152	1973	Hancocks S B Co, Pembroke Dock	Portsmouth/ Devonport/ Rosyth
GWENDO-LINE	A196	1973	" "	Rosyth
HELEN	A198	1974	" "	Portsmouth

RMAS Felicity

Length 72' **Beam** 21' **Draught** 8' 6" **GRT** 143 tons **Speed** 9.5 knots **Engines** Lister Blackstone ERS 8 MGR. **BHP** 615 **Propulsion** Single Voith Schneider Unit. **Bollard Pull** 5.68 tons **Range** 1000 miles @ 9.5 knots **Complement** 4.

Notes
Used to assist ships berthing and unberthing under their own power, assisting larger tugs with cold moves and towing lighters etc.

TWIN UNIT TRACTOR TUGS
ADEPT CLASS

Ship	Penn No.	Comp. Date	Builder	Based
ADEPT	A224	1980	R Dunston	Portsmouth
BUSTLER	A225	1981	" "	" "
CAPABLE	A226	1981	" "	Devonport/ Gibraltar
CAREFUL	A227	1982	" "	" "
FORCEFUL	A221	1985	" "	Devonport
NIMBLE	A222	1985	" "	Rosyth

Length 38.785m, 105′ 2″ **Beam** 9.41m, 30′ 10″ **Draught** 4.2m max, 13′ 9″ **GRT** 375 **Speed** 12.2 knots **Engines** Diesel, Ruston 6 RKCM x 2 **BHP** 2640 **Propulsion** Twin Voith Schneider Units **Bollard Pull** 29.63 tons **Range** 1500 miles @ 10 knots.

Notes
Designed for harbour work with sea towing, firefighting and salvage capabilities.

Replaced DIRECTOR Class paddle tugs and CONFIANCE Class screw tugs.

The bridge is designed to give maximum 'reflection free' visibility including upward visibility for working under ships with high freeboards.

Engine and towing winch controls are sited within the wheelhouse for direct control of towing operations.

RMAS Adept

Further tugs of this class to be built during 1985/6.

	Pennant No
POWERFUL	A223
FAITHFUL	A228
DEXTEROUS	A231

TUGS OPERATED BY ROYAL NAVAL ARMAMENT DEPOTS

ANCONA See page 20. Based Upnor, Chatham. Sold 1946.

BERING Diesel tug based Lake Timsah, Ismalia. Disposed of locally 1949.

BOMBSHELL See page 32. Based RNAD Bull Point, Plymouth. 1967 transferred to RNAD Coulport. February 1971 for sale at Greenock. 13.1.72 towed from Greenock to Hansweert (Holland).

BOOMERANG Built by Lobnitz & Co, Renfrew. 1945. **Length** 123′ 6″ **Beam** 24′ 6″ **Draught** 10′ 6″ Single screw. Oil fired. 2 holds with 100 ton cargo capacity. **Complement** 5 officers and 8 ratings. Based Hong Kong towing lighters and transporting armament stores. 1947 at Trincomalee for repairs . 19.9.50 sold to Messrs Henry P Lenahan & Sons, Hong Kong.

BRITON Built Falmouth 1905. **Length** 68′ 1″ **Beam** 14′ 2″. Hired from W J Reynolds and based Bull Point, Plymouth 1944.

CANNON Built by A Hall, Aberdeen 1944. **Length** 77′ 6″ **Beam** 19′ 6″ **GRT** 122. Steam tug, triple expansion engine single screw. **Complement** 2 officers, 6 ratings. Based RNAD Upnor, Chatham. 28.3.47 transferred to RNAD Priddys Hard, Portsmouth. 1.2.71 sold to H G Pounds, Portsmouth.

CARBINE Built by Yarwood & Son, Northwich, 1935. **Length** 90′ 6″ **Beam** 22′ 6″ **Draught** 9′ 2″ **GRT** 151. Steam triple expansion engine single screw. Coal fired. **IHP** 340 **Speed** 8 knots. **Range** 800 miles. Small hold—22 tons cargo capacity. Based Malta with locally entered civilian crew. Served at Alexandria during World War II. 23.3.59 transferred to Baileys, Malta.

CHAINSHOT	See page 32. Based RNAD Priddys Hard, Portsmouth. 4.9.46 transferred to Upnor, Chatham. 18.12.68 transferred to RNAD Coulport. 12.3.73 sold.
COCHIN	See page 20. Based RNAD, Bull Point, Plymouth. 20.2.47 sold to Anglo Danubian Transport Co Ltd.
CRAY	See page 142. Based Priddys Hard, Portsmouth.
EMPIRE WILLOW	See page 50. Based Bull Point, Plymouth 1945.
GRAPESHOT	See page 32. Based Upnor, Chatham. 5.3.74 sold.
GRAY	Steam tug. **Length** 72' **Beam** 18' 5" **Draught** 9' 6" **IHP** 370. **Complement** 2 officers, 5 ratings. Requisitioned 1943. Based Upnor, Chatham. 12.10.46 to D of ST for disposal.
KATHLEEN	Built by J S White & Co 1936. **Length** 60' **Beam** 15' 4". Diesel tug single screw. **BHP** 260. Requisitioned 1939 (with owner's crew) and based Upnor, Chatham. 28.3.47 returned to owners.
LADY STRICKLAND	Built Dartmouth 1913. **Length** 77' **Beam** 16' 6" **GRT** 59. Twin screw tug requisitioned and based at Malta during World War II. 1946 returned to owners.
LOCH LONG	Twin screw tug **IHP** 375. Based RN Torpedo Depot Malta. 1938 transferred to Singapore. September 1947 sunk at Singapore.
LUCY	Built Mordey Carney 1902. **Length** 78' **Beam** 16' 8" **Draught** 8' 6" **GRT** 140 **IHP** 200. Tug and cargo. Based Malta. 1937 sold.
MARCHWOOD	Built Dundee Shipbuilding Co 1901. **Length** 82' **Beam** 16' 6" Single screw **GRT** 140 **IHP** 200 **Speed** 7 knots. **Complement** 3 officers, 5 ratings. Based Lyness under DAS. 14.2.48 sold to James A White, Shipbreaking, North Queensferry.

MINION	See page 32. Based Priddys Hard, Portsmouth. 19.8.60 sold to H G Pounds, Portsmouth.
PATRICIA (MZINGA)	Steam tug. **Length** 41′ **Beam** 11′ 6″. December 1944 allocated to C in CEI Kilindini for DAS. 4.12.50 sold at Kilindini.
ROUNDSHOT	See page 32. Based Singapore. 5.6.69 sold to Siong Huat. Singapore.
STURDY No 10	**Length** 55′ **Beam** 12′ **Draught** 3′ 3″. Diesel tug **BHP** 100. On naval service Alexandria 1946.
STURDY No 21	As for No 10. 11.2.46 naval service Alexandria. 24.11.47 at RNAD Lake Timsah. 11.9.51 transferred to RNAD Kilindini. 5.11.54 for disposal locally.
STURDY No 30	As for No 10. 1946 at Port Said. 9.11.49 transferred to War Office.
TAMPEON	See page 24. Based Upnor, Chatham. 9.4.58 transferred to Priddys Hard. Portsmouth. 13.2.64 sold.
TRUNNION	See page 24. Based RNAD, Bull Point, Plymouth. 12.12.63 sold.
WAINSCOTT	Purchased 1919. Wooden Hull. **Length** 63′ **Beam** 16′ **Draught** 4′ 6″ **GRT** 58. Based Upnor, Chatham until 1943.
WEST BAY	See page 19. Based Priddys Hard, Portsmouth until 10.7.46 then C & M. 23.7.53 sold.

RNADs also operated TIDs, TANACs, a TUSA and 52½′ HLDs. Present day towage and conveyance of stores is carried out by vessels of the RMAS.

TUGS OPERATED BY NAVAL STORES DEPARTMENTS

C2 (VIGILANT)   Paddle tug. **Length** 80' 6" **Beam** 17' 6" **GRT** 115 **IHP** 340. Based Portsmouth until about 1940.

C9 (WEST ACRE)   See page 19. Based Portsmouth for Fleet Fuelling duties. 3.6.48 transferred to C D Portsmouth and reverted to original name WEST ACRE. 3.5.50 sold to Messrs E Handcock (1929) Ltd, Cardiff. 1960 sold again and renamed LAVEROCK.

C10 (DESTINY)   Built by Cochrane & Sons Ltd, Selby 1937. **Length** 80' **Beam** 21' Diesel engine **BHP** 450 **GRT** 89 **Speed** 10 knots. Based Portsmouth for Fleet Fuelling duties. 1958 named DESTINY. 13.11.63 sold to H G Pounds, Portsmouth.

C11 (REGARD)   Built by Cook, Welton & Gemmell Ltd 1938. **Length** 91' **Beam** 25' 3" **GRT** 143.98 Single screw steam tug—coal fired—70 tons, **IHP** 503 **Speed** 8 knots. Based Portsmouth for Fleet Fuelling duties. Originally FOREMOST 91 then C11 and renamed REGARD in 1959. 25.5.66 sold to Jos de Smedt, Antwerp.

Regard (1962)

C62 (HALLGARTH)	Built by Lytham S B. Purchased March 1900 **GRT** 175 **IHP** 240. Based Devonport for Fleet Fuelling duties until 1943 then sold.
C64 (FOREMOST)	Built by Cook, Welton & Gemmell Ltd 1938. **Length** 91' **Beam** 25' 3" Single screw, steam coal fired—70 tons. **GRT** 143.21 **IHP** 500 **Speed** 8 knots. Originally FOREMOST 90, then C64 then FOREMOST. Based Devonport for Fleet Fuelling duties. 24.10.67 sold to Jos de Smedt, Antwerp.
C102 (STOBO CASTLE) (W73)	Built by John Cran, Leith 1917. **Length** 110' 6" **Beam** 27' 5" **Draught** 12' **GRT** 280. Steam, coal fired—80 tons, single screw **IHP** 980. **Speed** 10 knots. Reinforced bow for ice breaking. Based Devonport for Fleet Fuelling duties. 8.8.63 sold to Jos de Smedt, Antwerp.
C108 (FLAMER)	Built by Scott, Bowling 1915. **Length** 18' 6" **Beam** 17' **Draught** 7' 6" **GRT** 124 **IHP** 250. Based Sheerness until about 1944. Became YC 298 in 1943. June 1948 sold to H G Pounds, Portsmouth.
C129	Built by Yarwood 1940. Single screw tug. **GRT** 46. Based Devonport. 17.2.55 sold to H Rose, Poole.
C150 (CARBON)	Built 1896. Purchased 1900. **GRT** 185 **IHP** 280. Based Portland. Sold 7.9.46.
C210 (VICTORY)	Built Falmouth 1900. Purchased 1904. **Length** 76.4' **Beam** 16' **Draught** 8.7' **GRT** 76 **IHP** 287. Based Malta until 1943.
C307	Built Portsmouth 1932. **Length** 108' **Beam** 24' **GRT** 192 **IHP** 300. Based Malta. September 1958 broken up by Virtu Co of Malta.
C308	As for C307. 11.5.42 sunk by mine off Malta.
C320 (WELSHMAN)	Built by Bow McLachlan, Paisley. **Length** 80' **Beam** 18' 6" **Draught** 10' 6" **GRT** 92 Steam—30 tons bunkers. **IHP** 330. **Speed** 11 knots. Purchased 1901. Based Gibraltar. 1947 sold.

C405	Built by Yarwood 1931. **Length** 86' **Beam** 22' **GRT** 134 **IHP** 480. Single screw steam tug—oil fired. Based Trincomalee 1944-1949,
C409 (SIR W JERVAISE)	Built Hong Kong 1900 for War Department. 1905 transferred to Admiralty and used as a tug. **Length** 99' **Beam** 18' **GRT** 120 **IHP** 330 **Speed** 10 knots. Based Hong Kong. 26.12.41 given to China or lost during Japanese occupation of Hong Kong.
C618	Built by A Hall, Aberdeen 1942. **Length** 84' **Beam** 24' **GRT** 158 **IHP** 400. Based Sheerness. 1958 sold to Hamilton Williams renamed ROBERT HAMILTON. 1959 sold to J H Lamey Ltd renamed EDITH LAMEY. 1966 converted to motor. 1969 sold to Oldham Bros, Liverpool, renamed MARTIN OLDFIELD. 1973 sold to Greece. Renamed HERMES.
C767 (SABU)	Built Holland. **Length** 78' **Beam** 18' **Draught** 9' **BHP** 320. Based Malta 1941. 11.4.49 numbered C767. 1958 transferred to C D and PAS manned. July 1963 sold to Salvatori Bezzina, Valletta. Renamed SABU.
C768 (LADY JANE)	Built by NSA Bacini, Naples 1944. **Length** 98' 7" **Beam** 24' 6" **Draught** 9' 6" **GRT** 221. Twin screws. Based Malta. 1946 replaced TUSA 221. January 1951 sold to United Commercial Industries & Maritime Co (Malta) Ltd and renamed BULL TERRIER.
CARMINA	Built Dordrecht 1915. **Length** 64' 8" **Beam** 14' 8" **Draught** 6' 8". Purchased by Lambert Bros, London for service in Gibraltar 1916. 29.11.39 purchased for the examination service—Gibraltar. On completion transferred to SNSO Gibraltar. 6.11.47 sold at Gibraltar.
DUKE	Used by Naval Stores Department, Greenock prior to 31.3.46 then to D of ST for disposal.

Hurricane

HURRICANE   Built by H Scarr, Hessle 1938. **Length** 78.5′ **Beam** 20.5′ **Draught** 8.4′ **GRT** 90 **BHP** 550. Single screw tug hired 29.11.39 as BBV. 1944 to Naval Stores Department Sheerness. January 1946 returned to owners James W Cook & Co Ltd. Still in service (1985) with Braithwaite and Dean Ltd, London.

LADY ELIZABETH   Built Holland 1927. **Length** 94.6′ **Beam** 21.6′ **Draught** 10.6′ **GRT** 165. Single screw tug. Entered naval service 1940. Based Portsmouth with Naval Store Department. 1945 returned to owners James Dredging & Towing Co, Southampton.

Naval Stores Departments also operated TANACs, TIDs & HLDs. Present day towage, conveyance of stores and Fleet Fuelling Service is carried out by RMAS vessels.

TUGS OPERATED BY DIRECTOR OF VICTUALLING

EMILY   Launched 28.11.01. Built by Seath, Rutherglen. **Length** 60' **Beam** 12' **Draught** 7.5' **GRT** 140 **IHP** 180. Based Malta. Sunk by aircraft 7.4.42.

ROBIN
REDBREAST   Built by J Pollock 1925. **Length** 62' **Beam** 16.1' **Draught** 6.4' **BHP** 280. Requisitioned and used at Royal William Victualling Yard, Plymouth. 12.6.46 Handed over to Messrs W D Tamlyn & Co.

USEFUL   Built by Philip & Son, Dartmouth 1935. **Length** 74' 6" **Beam** 16' **Draught** 5' 6" **GRT** 58.5. Steam—coal fired. **Range** 280 miles **Speed** 8 knots **IHP** 160. **Cargo Capacity** 12 tons. Based Portland until 1946 then to Royal Clarence Yard, Portsmouth. 10.11.59 sold to H G Pounds. Portsmouth.

Victualling yards also operated TIDs, TANACs & HLDs.

133

MISCELLANEOUS TUGS BASED IN HM DOCKYARDS AND NAVAL BASES

CHERUB Built by Hong Kong and Whampoa Shipyard 1901. **Length** 115' **Beam** 21' **GRT** 390 **IHP** 300. Steam tug and tank vessel based Hong Kong. December 1941 war loss.

CONQUERESS Built by Hepple 1913. Purchased 6.10.15. **Length** 95.9' **Beam** 20.1' **Draught** 9.8' **GRT** 240 **IHP** 700. Single screw steam tug based Portsmouth. 6.5.53 sold to Pollock & Brown, Northam for scrap.

ENTERPRISE (EMPRISE) Built by Bow McLachlan 1900. Twin screw. **Length** 110' **Beam** 23' **GRT** 300' **IHP** 450. Based Portsmouth. 1919 renamed EMPRISE. 1935 sold.

MARY TAVY (DANNY) Built by Philip & Son 1918. Twin screws. **Length** 93' 6" **Beam** 25' **Draught** 12' 6" **GRT** 162 **IHP** 800. Based Chatham under CD. July 1947 sold and renamed DANNY.

IMARA (PERSEVERANCE) Built by Fleming & Ferguson 1931. Purchased 1932. **Length** 116' 9" **Beam** 28' 6" **Draught** 13' **Displacement** 425 tons. Coal fired **IHP** 1100. **Speed** 11 knots **Range** 920 miles. Based Chatham under CD. 1958 sold to British Iron and Steel Corporation.

TUG 315 (PROMPT) Based Devonport 1934-44.

JASON (RIVAL) Built 1913. single screw. Purchased 5.2.15 **Length** 75' **Beam** 16' **Draught** 5' **GRT** 85 **Speed** 8.5 knots **IHP** 300. Based Chatham under CD as basin tug. 1937 renamed RIVAL. 1946 sold.

SPARKLER Built Yarwood, Northwich 1940. Single screw. **Length** 96' 6" **Beam** 23' **Draught** 9' **Displacement** 161 tons. Steam triple expansion engine **IHP** 500. Coal fired. Based Londonderry with HMS FERRET. Civilian manned under RFA conditions. **Complement** 4 officers, 5 ratings. 11.6.57 sold to Messrs J H Lamey Ltd, Liverpool.

Conqueress

UNITED STATES NAVAL RESCUE TUGS OPERATED DURING THE WAR UNDER THE LEND/LEASE AGREEMENT:—

Length 143' **Beam** 33' 3" **Draught** 13' 6" **Displacement** 783 tons **Speed** 14 knots **Engines** by General Motors, Diesel—electric drive **Fuel** Diesel 186 tons **HP** 1875 **Propulsion** Twin screws **Complement** 34.

Ship	Penn. No.	Comp. Date	Builder	Remarks
ADVANTAGE	W133	1942	Levingston	Ex USN ATR41 To commercial service 1946.
AIMWELL	W113	1942	Defoe	Ex USN BAT7 Sold 14.3.48.
ASPIRANT	W134	1943	Levingston	Ex USN ATR42 To commercial service 1948.
ATHLETE	W150	1943	" "	Ex USN ATR92. Lost 17.7.45. Mined off Leghorn.
BOLD	W114	1942	Defoe	Ex USN BAT8. Sold 2.10.48.
CHEERLY	W153	1943	Levingston	Ex USN ATR95. Returned to USN 19.2.46.
DESTINY	W115	1942	Defoe	Ex USN BAT9. To commercial service 1948.
EMINENT	W116	1942	Defoe	Ex USN BAT10. To commercial service 1946.
EMPHATIC	W154	1943	Levingston	Ex USN ATR96. To commercial service 1947.
FAVOURITE	W119	1942	" "	Ex USN BAT3. To commercial service 1946.
FLARE	W151	1943	" "	Ex USN ATR93. To commercial service 1946.

Ship	Penn. No.	Comp. Date	Builder	Remarks
FLAUNT	W152	1943	Levingston	Ex USN ATR94. To commercial service 1946.
INTEGRITY	W14	1942	" "	Ex USN BAT4. Returned to USN 19.2.46.
LARIAT	W17	1942	" "	Ex USN BAT5. To commercial service 1946.
MASTERFUL	W20	1942	" "	Ex USN BAT6. To commercial service 1948.
MINDFUL	W135	1943	" "	Ex USN ATR48. Some service in Mediterranean. Returned to USN 13.5.46.
ORIANA	W117	1943	Gulfport. Engines by Allis Chalmers	Ex USN BAT1. To commercial service 1946.
PATROCLUS	W118	1943	Levingston	Ex USN ATR91. To commercial service 1947.
RESERVE	W149	1942	" "	Ex USN BAT11. RAN 1944.
SPRIGHTLY	W103	1942	" "	Ex USN BAT12. RAN. 1944.
TANCRED	W104	1943	Gulfport	Ex USN BAT13. RAN 1944.
VAGRANT	W136	1943	Levingston	Ex USN ATR49. To commercial service 1947.
WEAZEL	W120	1943	Gulfport	Ex USN BAT14. To commercial service 1946.

USN HARBOUR TUGS ON LEND/LEASE

Length 102′ 3″ **Beam** 24′ **Draught** 10′ **Displacement** 300 tons **Speed** 12 knots **Engines** Diesel—electric drive **BHP** 1000 **Propulsion** Single screw.

Ship	Comp. Date	Builder	Remarks
BUSY	1942	Gulfport	Ex USN BYT 1. Returned to USN January 1947.
CONFIDENT	1942	″ ″	Ex USN BYT 2. Returned to USN 1946.
HELPFUL	1942	″ ″	Ex USN BYT 3.
INTENT	1942	″ ″	Ex USN BYT 4.
RESOLUTE	1942	″ ″	Ex USN BYT 5.

Served as rescue tugs in the West Indies, Mediterranean and with the Eastern Fleet.

WOODEN HULL TUGS

Length 165' **Beam** 34' **Draught** 16' **Displacement** 1360 tons **Speed** 12 knots **Engines** Steam triple expansion—2 watertube boilers. **Fuel** FFO 220 tons **IHP** 1875 **Propulsion** Single screw **Complement** 32.

Ship	Penn. No.	Comp. Date	Builder	Remarks
DIRECTOR	W137	1943	Camden	Ex USN BATR 17. Returned to USN 23.4.46.
EMULOUS	W138	1943	" "	Ex USN BATR 18. Returned to USN 30.4.46.
FREEDOM	W139	1943	" "	Ex USN BATR 19. Returned to USN 23.4.46.
JUSTICE	W140	1943	" "	Ex USN BATR 20. To commercial service 1948.

TUSA CLASS
Wood built in USA. Lend/Lease. The class name is thought to be derived from Tug-USA.
Length 65' **Beam** 18' 8" **Engine** Diesel **HP** 240.
Notes

TUSA 219	March 1946. At Malta with CD awaiting spares from USA. 1.2.47 in poor condition and for disposal. April 1947 returned to the American office of the Foreign Liquidation Commissioner—Lend/Lease Craft.
TUSA 220 and 221	As for 219.
TUSA 224	5.6.45 allocated to C in CBPF Sydney. 11.3.46 in C & M pending disposal. 8.9.48 sold through Australian Commonwealth Disposal Board.
TUSA 226	As for 224.
TUSA 227	As for 224.

Tusa 220

TUSA 230	13.10.44 arrived Sydney—allocated to C in CBPF. Nominal Base Ship at Sydney HMS GOLDEN HIND. 4.9.48 sold through Australian Commonwealth Disposal Board.
TUSA 231	8.3.45 allocated to C in CEI at Bombay. 9.6.45 at Trincomalee under FO Ceylon and used by Naval Armament Supply Officer. 31.8.46 lifted in HMS EASTWAY to Singapore. August 1947 sold to Robin & Co, Singapore.
TUSA 232	28.8.44 arrived Sydney allocated to C in CBPF. 2.10.47 sold through Australian Commonwealth Disposal Board.
TUSA 233	8.3.45 allocated to C in CEI at Bombay. 17.4.45 at Trincomalee and sailed for Rangoon. Transferred to Burma RNVR. 1947 sold by Government of Burma as scrap.
TUSA 234	28.8.44 Arrived Sydney allocated to C in CBPF. 5.6.45 at Brisbane. 2.10.47 sold through Australian Commonwealth Disposal Board.

TUGS ACQUIRED FOR SERVICE DURING WORLD WAR II—AND WAR PRIZES

ABEILLE 4
(French) (W94)
Built 1939 **GRT** 327 Requisitioned 1940—
served at Aberdeen, Dundee & Milford
Haven. Returned 1946

ABEILLE 5
(French)
Built 1910 **GRT** 211 Requisitioned 1940
minewatching service at Plymouth.
Returned 1946

ABEILLE 20
(French)
Built 1910 **GRT** 179 Requisitioned 1940
for MWT. Returned 1945

ABEILLE 21
(French)
Built 1925 **GRT** 260 Requisitioned 1940
for service as Rescue Tug. Returned 1945

ABEILLE 22
(ex St MINVER)
(French)
Built 1919 **GRT** 433 Requisitioned 1940
for MWT. Returned 1945

ALHATHERA
(ex KIFARU)
Built 1927 **GRT** 279 Requisitioned 1939
Returned 1945

ALLEN
Twin screw tug based Portland
Requisitioned 7.6.41 Returned 27.7.45

AMSTERDAM
(Netherlands)
Built 1937 **GRT** 368 Requisitioned 1939
Returned 1945

ATTENTIF
(French) (W68)
Built 1938 **GRT** 672 Requisitioned 1940—
served at Aberdeen, Milford Haven &
Harwich. Returned 1945

BALNA
Built Haarlem, Holland 1929. **Length** 54.6′
Beam 14.6′ **Draught** 6.2′ **GRT** 88 **BHP** 200.
Single screw diesel tug based Gibraltar.
Requisitioned at Gibraltar October 1942.
Sold 1.10.46.

BAT (ex
BRAHMAN)
Built by Cochrane & Sons, Selby 1938.
Length 101.1′ **Beam** 20.1′ **GRT** 230. Owned
and manned by United Towing Co, Hull. At
Rosyth 26.8.39 to 27.1.45.

BERMUDIAN
Built 1919. **HP** 1150. Tug requisitioned from
Messrs Furness & Whitby Ltd, for service at
Bermuda. Returned 1948.

BRITON
Built Falmouth 1905. **Length** 68′ **Beam** 14′
2″. Hired from W J Reynolds and based
Bull Point, Plymouth 1944.

CALSHOT	Built 1930 **GRT** 679. Requisitioned 1940. Returned 1946.
CANUTE	Built by Thorneycroft 1922. **GRT** 271 **Length** 111.5′ **Beam** 29.7′ **IHP** 1200. Twin screw tug based Portsmouth Requisitioned 1.7.41 Returned 18.8.45.
CAPTIVE (ex MAX BARENDT) (W148)	Built 1923 **GRT** 766 ex German tug scuttled at Alexandria and salvaged by RN in 1942. Sunk at Potomas Bay 3.2.46.
CAROLINE MOLLER (ex St MABYN) (W09)	Built 1919. **GRT** 444 Requisitioned 1940 Lost 7.10.42. Torpedoed by E Boat in the North Sea.
CERVIA	Built 1925 **GRT** 157 Requisitioned 1941 returned 1945
CHAMPION (French) (W35)	Built 1939. **Displacement** 672 Requisitioned 1940 for service at Dundee. Returned 1945
CHERBOURGE- OIS I (French)	Built 1903 **GRT** 90 seized 1940 returned May 1945.
CHERBOURGE- OIS III (French) (W99)	Built 1913 **GRT** 281 Seized at Poole 3.7.40 for service as rescue tug. Returned 1946.
CHERBOURGE- OIS IV (French) (W107)	Built 1930 **GRT** 293 Seized at Plymouth 3.7.40. Twin screws tug based Devonport under CD. Returned April 1946.
COBURG	Built 1934 **GRT** 201 Requisitioned 25.8.39. Returned 14.10.40. Based Devonport under CD.
CORINGA	Built 1914 **GRT** 294 Requisitioned 1939 Lost 23.6.40. in North Atlantic.
CRAY	Built Philip & Son, Dartmouth 1913. **Length** 72′ **Beam** 18′ 6″ **GRT** 72. Single screw Requisitioned 1940 based Priddys Hard, Portsmouth with RNAD. 18.6.46 to D of ST for disposal.
DAISY	Foundered on passage from Alexandria to Tobruk 2.1.42.
DANUBE III	Built 1924 **GRT** 234 Requisitioned 1939. Used in the Examination Service. Lost 13.10.40. mined off Sheerness.

DANUBE V (W36)	Built 1935 **GRT** 241 Requisitioned 1939. Returned 1945. Steam tug of **IHP** 900 used in the Examination Service.
DANUBE VI	Built 1935 **GRT** 241 Requisitioned 1939. Returned 1945. Steam tug of **IHP** 900. Used in the Examination Service.
DART	Built 1928. Returned 1946. Diesel tug **BHP** 120. Used as Basin Tug at Sheerness.
DIPPER	Built Hamburg 1943 as C30. **Length** 88′ 10″ OA **Beam** 16′ 6″ **Draught** 9′ 8″ **GRT** 102.21 Diesel **BHP** 375. **Speed** 9 knots. Push button steering. Ex German mine location vessel seized as a prize. RN manned and attached to HMS LOCHINVAR, Port Edgar. About 1958 to PAS Rosyth. 1963 to Singapore.
DIVER	Built Hamburg 1943 as C28. As for DIPPER. Allocated to HMS LOCHINVAR, Port Edgar and naval manned. 1958 replaced TID 83 at Chatham. 1961 transferred to Rosyth to replace TID 165. 1963 towed by WARDEN to Plymouth. September 1963 towed by ADVICE to Singapore. 3.4.71 transferred to Singapore Government.

HM Tug Diver (Sept 1951)

DIVETTE	Seized 3.7.40 at Southampton. 1941-45 at Belfast. 1945 returned.
DIVERSION (ex NORMAN)	Built 1929 **GRT** 222 Requisitioned 1939. Returned 1943.
DROMEDARY	Built 1911. Single screw tug believed to be ex Belgian tug PRESIDENT ARNARD GRISAR. **IHP** 220. Purchased March 1940. Based Sheerness. 6.10.47 sold to F W Payne, Canvey Island.
DUKE	Used by Naval Stores Dept. Greenock prior to 31.3.46 then to D of ST for disposal.
DUNDAS	Built by Degrot & Van Flet, Holland. 1919. **Length** 119′ **Beam** 23′ **GRT** 254. Owned and manned by Grangemouth & Forth Towing Co and used as required for the movements of ships at Rosyth during the war years.
EASTWICK	Acquired for naval service 24.4.44 and allocated to C in CEI at Trincomalee. 14.10.48 beyond economical repair. 1950 disposed of as a wreck during Trincomalee harbour clearance.
ELAN II (French)	Seized 3.7.40 at Southampton. After service as Barrage Balloon vessel at Sheerness served at Devonport 1941-45 as Target Towing tug.
ELIE (ex INGLEAY CROSS)	Built by J T Eltringham & Co, South Shields, 1912. Paddle tug. **Length** 168′ **Beam** 21′ **GRT** 168. Owned and manned by Grangemouth & Forth Towing Co. Served at Rosyth Dockyard 1940-45.
ENGLISHMAN	Built 1937 **GRT** 487. Requisitioned 1939. Sunk by a/c 21.1.41.
EVERARD	Built 1928 **Length** 92′ **Beam** 22′ 6″ **Draught** 11′ 6″ **HP** 850. Based Chatham under CD. Returned to owners 22.2.46 and replaced by EXPELLER.
EXCALIBUR (ex FINKEN WARDER)	German tug allocated to UK 1945. Reallocated to Russia by Tripartite Naval Commission.

Excluder (April 1948)

EXCLUDER (ex GOLDINGEN)	Built 1942 by Wartsila Concernen A B Finland **Length** 152′ **Beam** 30′ **Draught** 9′ 6″ **GRT** 539.56. Twin screws. Steam recip. engines **IHP** 900. Coal fired. Kort Nozzle, twin rudders. German tug seized 1945. Based Portsmouth Dockyard under CD. 2.8.50 for sale. 1958 sold and renamed LENADIL.
EXHORTER (ex OSTPREUSSEN)	Built 1942. Sister ship to EXCLUDER. Seized 1945. Based Devonport under CD. 1962 sold to H G Pounds, Portsmouth. 21.12.63 towed from Portsmouth to Malta by Dutch tug LOIRE.
EXPELLER (ex BORA)	Built by Nobiskrug GMBH Germany 1942. German single screw tug seized 1945. Diesel engine by Motorenwerke, Mannheim AG **BHP** 820. **GRT** 317.11. Allocated to C D Chatham to replace EVERARD. 1967 replaced by MASTIFF. 18.10.68 sold to Salvatori Bezzina, Malta. Renamed SABI.

EXPLOITER (ex MELLUM)	Built 1942. **GRT** 106. 1.12.45 on naval service. 1946 on harbour service for HMS FERRET at Londonderry. 2.12.46 Allocated to American Forces by D of ST.
EXTIRPER (ex MARIENBURG)	German tug built 1944. Diesel engine **BHP** 1200. Allocated to UK by Allied Commission but chartered to Netherlands Government. 10.3.47 transferred to Netherlands Government.
EXUBERANT (ex SCHULAU)	German tug allocated to UK in 1945 for naval service at Harwich. 13.5.46 reallocated to Russia by Tripartite Commission. Relieved by EMPIRE LUCY.
FABIA	Built 1919 **GRT** 151 Requisitioned 1939. Returned 1945.
FAIRPLAY TWO	Built 1921 **GRT** 282 Requisitioned 1939 Lost 2.3.40 wrecked off Yorkshire coast.
FALCON (W129)	Built 1892 **GRT** 124 Requisitioned 1941. Returned 1945.
FAWLEY	Built Northwich 1915. **Length** 68′ 4″ **Beam** 15′ 6″. Single screw tug based Portsmouth. Hired from James Dredging, Towage & Transport Co 1944.
FLYFISH	Built 1882. Paddle tug. **Length** 116′ **Beam** 19′ 6″ **GRT** 169. Owned and manned by Leith Salvage & Towing Co and served at Rosyth Dockyard 1940-45.
FORCEFUL (W126)	Built 1925 **GRT** 288 Requisitioned 1941 Returned 1944.
GOLIATH (Belgian) (W121)	Built 1921 **GRT** 354 Requisitioned 1940 Returned 1945.
GONDIA	Paddle tug. Built 1927 **GRT** 200 Requisitioned 1940 Returned 1946.
GRANGEBURN	Built by Grangemouth Dkyd Co 1937. **GRT** 196. **Length** 100′ **Beam** 24.9′. Single screw steam tug **IHP** 900. Owned and manned by Grangemouth & Forth Towing Co and used as required for movements of ships at Rosyth Dockyard during the war years. Returned 19.11.45.

GRAY	See page 127. Requisitioned 1943. Returned 1946.
GUARDSMAN	Built 1905 **GRT** 102 Requisitioned 1939. Lost 15.11.40 mined off North Foreland.
HENDON	Built 1924 **GRT** 241 Requisitioned 1940 Returned 1942.
HENRIETTE MOLLER	Fleet Tug 1942-45. Far East.
HUDSON (Netherlands (W02)	Built 1939 **GRT** 294 Requisitioned 1940 Returned 1946.
HURRICANE	See page 132.
HYADES (ex TAURUS)	Italian prize. **HP** 400. With CD Alexandria. Returned 1946.
INDIRA	Built 1918 **GRT** 637 Requisitioned 1940 Lost 15.12.41 sunk by aircraft at Hong Kong.
ISERE (French)	Built 1919 **GRT** 107. Aug 1940-45. Harbour Tug at Dartmouth. 1945 Returned.
JAMES E HUGHES	Built 1914 **GRT** 293 Requisitioned 1943 Returned 1946.
JAVA	Built 1918 **GRT** 155 Requisitioned 1940 Returned 1945. Based at Londonderry.
JOBURG (French)	Seized 3.7.40 at Southampton. 1940-45 at Larne, Belfast & Plymouth—Target towing.
KATHLEEN	See page 127.
KENIA (W47)	Built 1927 **GRT** 200 Requisitioned 1939 Returned 1945.
KERSE	Built by Cran & Sommerville, Leith. **Length** 100.1′ **Beam** 24′ **GRT** 214. Owned and manned by Grangemouth & Forth Towing Co and used as required for the movements of ships in Rosyth Dockyard during the war years.
KESTREL II	Built 1918 **GRT** 161 Requisitioned 1940 Returned 1945. Used as Boom Defence tender.
KROOMAN	Built by Cochrane & Sons, Selby 1938. Single screw **HP** 800. **Length** 100.1′ **Beam** 20.1′ **GRT** 230. Owned and manned by United Towing Co, Hull. Served at Rosyth 1939-45.

LA PERNELLE	1941-45 Examination & Harbour duty at Londonderry. Returned 1945.
LADY BRASSEY	Built 1913 **GRT** 362 Requisitioned 1939 Returned 1946.
LADY CECILA	Served at Rosyth 1939-45. Owned and manned by Leith Salvage & Towing Co.
LADY ELIZABETH	See page 132.
LADY JANE (C768)	See page 131.
MAINE	Requisitioned tug. At Gibraltar 28.12.45, Malta 17.2.47. Hong Kong 5.12.49 and at Singapore 30.1.50.
MAMMOUTH (French) (W56)	Built 1918 Dis 954 tons. Requisitioned 1943 Returned 1946.
MASTODONTE (French) (W70)	Built 1919 Dis 954 tons. Requisitioned 1939 Returned 1945.
MERRY MOLLER	Built 1926 **GRT** 382. March 1946 at Shanghai used for berthing and passenger carrying.
MIU	Single screw tug based Gibraltar 1945.
MURIA	Built 1914 **GRT** 192 Requisitioned 1939 Lost 8.11.40, mined off North Foreland.
NAPIA	Built 1914 **GRT** 155 Requisitioned 1939 Lost 20.12.39 off Ramsgate—probably mined.
NESS POINT	Built 1937 **GRT** 85 Requisitioned 1940 Returned 1946.
NEYROU	**Length** 132′ **Beam** 24′ **Draught**12′ 6″. Steam recip. **IHP** 750. Based at Shatt el Arab under C in CEI 1943.
NGUVU	Built 1925 **GRT** 179 Requisitioned 1939 Returned 1945. With Kenya and Zanzibar RNVR. Returned to East Africa Railways & Harbour Board.
NORMAN	Built by Cochrane & Sons, Selby 1938. Single screw. **Length** 100.1′ **Beam** 20.1′ **GRT** 230 **IHP** 800. Owned and manned by United Towing Co, Hull. Served at Rosyth 1939-45.
PENFELD	French tug seized 3.7.40 at Devonport. **IHP** Approx 900. Based Devonport under CD. Returned 1946.

PETREL IV (French)	Built 1932 **GRT** 80. Single screw diesel tug, used as seaplane tender, seized at Portsmouth 1940. Returned 27.4.45.
PEUPLIER (French)	Seized 1940 at Plymouth for Harbour Service. 30.4.41 sunk near Plymouth.
PINGOUIN (French)	Built 1917 Dis 700 tons. Requisitioned 1943 Returned 1945.
PINTARD (French)	Built 1917 Dis 700 tons. Requisitioned 1943 Returned 1945.
PRIMA (W 95)	Built Northwich 1930. **Length** 55.1′ **Beam** 15.1′. Single screw tug based Portsmouth with SCE as W95.
RAMIER (French)	Built 1917 Dis 685 tons. Requisitioned 1943 Returned 1945.
REINA VICTORIA	Built Glasgow 1908. **GRT** 59. Requisitioned August 1941. Based Gibraltar under CD. 1.5.47 to Shell Co.
RENE LE BESNERAIS (French)	Built 1931 **GRT** 246. Requisitioned 1943 Returned 1945.
REVUE (W62)	Built by Cochrane & Sons, Selby 1939. **Length** 105.1′ **Beam** 26.6′ **GRT** 274. Twin screws. Served at Rosyth 1939-45. Owned by Beira Works Ltd.
RISBAN	Built 1924 **GRT** 159. Requisitioned 1940 Returned 1946.
ROBIN REDBREAST	See page 133.
ROODE ZEE (Netherlands) (W162)	Built 1938 **GRT** 468 Requisitioned 1940. Lost 24.4.44, torpedoed by E Boat off Dungeness.
SABINE (W74)	Built 1917 **GRT** 488. Purchased in USA 1940. Scrapped at Gateshead 1950.
SAINT DOMINIC	Built 1919 **GRT** 451. Requisitioned 1939. Lost 8.12.41 in China Sea.
SAINT OLAVES	Built 1919 **GRT** 468. Requisitioned 1939. Lost 21.9.42 wrecked near Duncansby Head.
SALVAGE KING	Built 1925 **GRT** 1164. Requisitioned 1940. Lost 12.9.40 wrecked near Duncansby Head.
SALVONIA (W43)	Built 1939 **GRT** 571. Requisitioned 1939. Returned 1945.

SAUCY	Built 1918 **GRT** 579. Requisitioned 1939. Lost 4.9.40 mined in Firth of Forth.
SAXON	Under C in C Med at Port Said. Returned 1945.
SCHELDE (Netherlands) (W156)	Built 1926 **GRT** 359. Requisitioned 1940 Returned 1945.
SCOTTIE	Built Faversham 1930. **Length** 65.8' **Beam** 16.2' **GRT** 50. Single screw diesel tug. **BHP** 270. Requisitioned 16.10.42. Based Gibraltar under CD. 28.3.46 shipped in S S SANTUCKY to Liverpool for disposal by D of ST. Scrapped 1969.
SCYTHE (ex BALTIC) (Belgian)	Built 1915 **Length** 79.3' **Beam** 19.6' **IHP** 450. Purchased 12.2.40 and based at Sheerness. 20.5.47 sold to Messrs E A & H Sandford and sailed under tow for Gravesend.
SEA GEM	Built 1939 **GRT** 92 Missing presumed lost 30.10.40.
SEA GIANT (W125)	Built 1920 Ex USN CONTOCOOK **GRT** 508 Purchased in USA 1940. Sold May 1948.
SEA MAN (W44)	Built 1924 **GRT** 369. Requisitioned 1939. Returned 1945.
SIR BEVOIS	Built by Day, Summers, Southampton 1916 **Length** 130.2' **Beam** 25.1'. Requisitioned (with crew) from Southampton and based Devonport under CD. Sunk at Millbay Docks during air raid on Plymouth.
SUN II	Built 1909 **GRT** 197. Requisitioned 1939 Returned 1945.
SUN III	Built 1909 **GRT** 197. Requisitioned 1939 Returned 1945.
SUN V	Built 1915 Steam recip. **GRT** 200 **IHP** 750 Requisitioned 1939 Returned 1945.
SUN VI	Built 1902 **HP** 450. Based Sheerness under CD. Returned 1945.
SUN VII	Built 1917 **GRT** 202. Requisitioned 1939. Lost 6.3.41 mined in Thames estuary.
SUN VIII	Built 1919 steam recip **IHP** 750 **GRT** 196. Requisitioned 1939 Returned 1946.

SUN IX	Built 1920 **GRT** 196. Requisitioned 1939. Lost 6.3.41 mined in Thames estuary.
SUN XII	Built 1925 Steam recip **IHP** 750 **GRT** 183. Requisitioned 1942 Returned 1945
SUNBIRD	Built 1907 **Length** 80′ **Beam** 19′ **Draught** 10′ **HP** 350. Basin tug at Chatham 1944 Returned 1946.
SUNFISH	Built 1907 **Length** 80′ **Beam** 19′ **Draught** 10′ **HP** 350. Basin tug at Chatham 1944 Returned 1946.
SUPERMAN (W89)	Built 1933 **GRT** 359. Requisitioned 1939 Returned 1945.
TACTFUL	Built 1909 Steam recip **IHP** 400 **GRT** 112 Hired from W J Reynolds for CD Devonport for a short period 1941.
TAURUS	Built 1931 **GRT** 107 tons. Single screw Italian prize, salvaged (probably at Massawa) and based Alexandria. Renamed HYADES 1943. Returned to owners 26.4.46.
THAMES (Netherlands)	Built 1938 **GRT** 624. Requisitioned 1940 Returned 1945.
TIEN HSING	Foundered in Red Sea on passage to Massawa 26.10.43.
TWENTE	Built 1937 **GRT** 239. Requisitioned 1940. Lost 12.6.40 cause unknown.
VICTOR	Built 1898 **GRT** 153. Requisitioned 1939. Returned 1945
VIRGINIA P	Based Malta under CD 18.7.46. Returned 1946.
WAPPING	Built 1936 **GRT** 201. Requisitioned from Liverpool (with crew) and based Devonport under CD. Returned 8.10.40.
WAREE (RAN) (W128)	Built 1939 **GRT** 233. Requisitioned 1942. Returned 1946
WATERMEYER (ex T H WATERMEYER)	Built 1939 **GRT** 621. Requisitioned 1939. Returned 1940. Twin screw tug, Returned to South African Railways & Harbour Board.
WATO (RAN) (W127)	Built 1904 **GRT** 292. Requisitioned 1941. Returned 1946.

WHITBURN	Paddle tug, built by G P Rennolson & Sons, South Shields, **Length** 95′ **Beam** 19′ **GRT** 119 **IHP** 250. Owned & manned by Grangemouth & Forth Towing Co and served at Rosyth 1940-45.
WILLIAM RYAN	Built 1928 **GRT** 102. Requisitioned 1939 Returned 1945.
WO KWANG	Built 1927 **GRT** 350. Lost at Singapore February 1942.
YIN PING	Built 1914. Sunk by gunfire 15.2.42.
ZWARTE ZEE (Netherlands) (W163)	Built 1933 **GRT** 793. Requisitioned 1940 Returned 1945.

TUGS IN CAMERA . . .

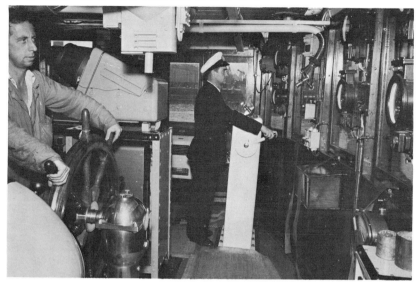

A view from the bridge . . . of a Confiance class tug

& from the towing winch.

The Navy's tugs have always pushed—or pulled—its largest and smallest ships.

Here, HM Tug St Clears tows a string of 32′ cutters to the Dunkirk beaches . . .

Whilst HMS Unicorn is eased alongside at Devonport (17 Nov 1953) by three of the local tugs.

154

HMS Forth arrives in Malta. As ever a tug (Robust) stands by to assist her to her berth—at buoys.

Every tow has a different characteristic. Here an Admiralty Floating dock is prepared for a coastal tow. If the weather worsens they have a habit of being somewhat unwieldy!

INDEX

156

DAISY (1)	101	EMPIRE BRACKEN	50	EMPIRE MINOTAUR	36
DAISY (2)	142	EMPIRE CADET	50	EMPIRE MUSTANG	50
DALMATIAN	96	EMPIRE CEDAR	35	EMPIRE NAN	50
DANUBE III	142	EMPIRE CHARLES	35	EMPIRE NED	36
DANUBE V	143	EMPIRE CHERUB	50	EMPIRE NETTA	36
DANUBE VI	143	EMPIRE CHRISTOPHER	35	EMPIRE NICHOLAS	36
DANNY	134	EMPIRE CLARA	50	EMPIRE NICHOLSON	35
DAPHNE	101	EMPIRE CONNIE	35	EMPIRE NINA	50
DART	143	EMPIRE CUPID	35	EMPIRE NORA	50
DASHOUND	67	EMPIRE DARBY	35	EMPIRE OAK	50
DECISION	25	EMPIRE DARLING	50	EMPIRE OBERON	36
DEERHOUND	96	EMPIRE DEMON	35	EMPIRE PALM	50
DESTINY (1)	129	EMPIRE DENIS	35	EMPIRE PAM	50
DESTINY (2)	136	EMPIRE DOLLY	50	EMPIRE PAT	36
DEXTEROUS (1)	25	EMPIRE DORIS	35	EMPIRE PAUL	50
DEXTEROUS (2)	117	EMPIRE DOROTHY	35	EMPIRE PEGGY	36
DEXTEROUS (3)	124	EMPIRE EDWARD	36	EMPIRE PERCY	50
DILIGENT (1)	25	EMPIRE ELINOR	50	EMPIRE PHYLLIS	36
DILIGENT (2)	38	EMPIRE FAIRY	35	EMPIRE PIERROT	37
DILIGENT (3)	110	EMPIRE FARM	35	EMPIRE PINE	50
DIPPER	143	EMPIRE FIR	50	EMPIRE PIPER	37
DIRECTOR (1)	117	EMPIRE FLORA	50	EMPIRE PIXIE	50
DIRECTOR (2)	139	EMPIRE FOLK	50	EMPIRE PLANE	37
DIVER (1)	143	EMPIRE FRANK	50	EMPIRE POLLY	50
DIVERSION	144	EMPIRE FRED	35	EMPIRE RACE	37
DIVETTE	144	EMPIRE FREDA	35	EMPIRE RAYMOND	50
DORIS	101	EMPIRE GNOME	35	EMPIRE RITA	37
DOROTHY (1)	42	EMPIRE GOBLIN	50	EMPIRE RODERICK	37
DOROTHY (2)	101	EMPIRE GRETA	50	EMPIRE ROGER	37
DRIVER	30	EMPIRE GRIFFIN	35	EMPIRE ROSA	37
DROMEDARY (1)	110	EMPIRE HARLEQUIN	35	EMPIRE RUPERT	50
DROMEDARY (2)	144	EMPIRE HARRY	50	EMPIRE RUTH	37
DUKE	131, 144	EMPIRE HELEN	50	EMPIRE SALLY	50
DUNDAS	144	EMPIRE HENCHMAN	50	EMPIRE SAM	37
		EMPIRE HILDA	50	EMPIRE SAMSON	37
E A EVERARD	62	EMPIRE HUMPHREY	35	EMPIRE SANDY	50
EARNER	25	EMPIRE IMP	35	EMPIRE SARA	50
EARNEST	25	EMPIRE IVY	35	EMPIRE SERAPH	37
EASTWICK	144	EMPIRE JANE	35	EMPIRE SHIELA	50
EDITH	101	EMPIRE JEAN	50	EMPIRE SHIRLEY	37
EDITH LAMEY	131	EMPIRE JENNY	35	EMPIRE SILAS	50
EGERTON	40	EMPIRE JESTER	50	EMPIRE SIMON	50
ELAN II	144	EMPIRE JOAN	36	EMPIRE SINEW	50
ELF	39	EMPIRE JOHN	36	EMPIRE SOPHY	37
EL GADIR	42	EMPIRE JONATHAN	36	EMPIRE SPITFIRE	37
ELIE	144	EMPIRE JOSEPHINE	36	EMPIRE SPRITE	50
ELKHOUND	96	EMPIRE JULIA	50	EMPIRE SPRUCE	37
EMERSON K	22	EMPIRE JUNA	50	EMPIRE STELLA	50
EMILY	133	EMPIRE KATY	36	EMPIRE STORMCOCK	50
EMINENT (1)	49	EMPIRE LARCH	36	EMPIRE SUSAN	50
EMINENT (2)	136	EMPIRE LAWN	36	EMPIRE SYBIL	50
EMPHATIC (1)	43	EMPIRE LEONARD	50	EMPIRE TEAK	37
EMPHATIC (2)	136	EMPIRE LEWIS	50	EMPIRE TESSA	37
EMPIRE ACE	34	EMPIRE LILLIPUT	50	EMPIRE THISTLE	50
EMPIRE AID	50	EMPIRE LINDEN	36	EMPIRE TITAN	37
EMPIRE ALFRED	50	EMPIRE LOLA	36	EMPIRE TITANIA	37
EMPIRE ANDREW	50	EMPIRE LUCY	36	EMPIRE TOBY	50
EMPIRE ANN	34	EMPIRE MADGE	36	EMPIRE VERA	50
EMPIRE ARIEL	34	EMPIRE MAID	50	EMPIRE VINCENT	37
EMPIRE ASH	50	EMPIRE MAISIE	50	EMPIRE WALTER	50
EMPIRE BARBARA	34	EMPIRE MAPLE	50	EMPIRE WARLOCK	50
EMPIRE BECKY	50	EMPIRE MARTHA	50	EMPIRE WILLOW	37
EMPIRE BELLE	34	EMPIRE MARY	50	EMPIRE WINNIE	50
EMPIRE BEN	35	EMPIRE MASCOT	36	EMPIRE WOLD	50
EMPIRE BESS	50	EMPIRE MEAD	36	EMPIRE ZONA	37
EMPIRE BETSY	50	EMPIRE MEADOW	50	EMPRISE	134
EMPIRE BIRCH	50	EMPIRE MINNOW	36	EMULOUS (1)	49